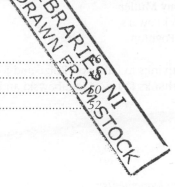

Section Four — Structure and Language

Section Five — Context and Critical Responses

Section Six — Writing About 'The Great Gatsby'

Published by CGP

Editors:
Claire Boulter
Holly Corfield-Carr
Josephine Gibbons
Anthony Muller
Rachael Powers
Holly Poynton

With thanks to Luke von Kotze and John Sanders for the proofreading.
With thanks to Laura Jakubowski and Laura Stoney for the copyright research.

Acknowledgements:

With thanks to Photofest for permission to reproduce the photograph on the front cover.
Paramount/Photofest © Paramount Pictures

Image on page 1: F. Scott Fitzgerald (1896-1940) (b/w photo) by American Photographer, (20th century)
Private Collection/ Roger-Viollet, Paris / The Bridgeman Art Library

With thanks to TopFoto for permission to use the images on page 1 © The Granger Collection / TopFoto

With thanks to Alamy for permission to use the images on pages 2 and 7.

With thanks to Photofest for permission to use the images on page 3.

With thanks to Rex Features for permission to use the images on pages 3, 4, 23, 26, 34, 54, 57, 58 and 60.

Images on pages 3 and 4 © FAMOUS PLAYERS / LASKY / THE KOBAL COLLECTION

Images on pages 3, 5, 10, 13, 15, 17, 19, 21, 24, 28, 30, 32, 36, 41, 45, 46, 51 and 53
© PARAMOUNT / THE KOBAL COLLECTION

With thanks to akg-images for permission to use the images on pages 5 and 8.

With thanks to The Moviestore Collection for permission to use the image on page 39.

With thanks to Suki Maltby-Duggan for permission to use the image on page 42.

With thanks to Mary Evans Picture Library for permission to use the image on page 48.

ISBN: 978 1 84762 668 4
Website: www.cgpbooks.co.uk
Printed by Elanders Ltd, Newcastle upon Tyne.
Clipart from CorelDRAW®

Based on the classic CGP style created by Richard Parsons.

F. Scott Fitzgerald and 'The Great Gatsby'

'The Great Gatsby' is a Very Influential Novel

1) The Great Gatsby is a **novel** about a **working-class man** who goes to great lengths to become **rich** and **win back** the woman he **loves**. She eventually **rejects** him in favour of someone of her **own class**, and he dies **alone**.

2) Gatsby's **failure** suggests that people **can't** reinvent themselves or **break away** from their **social class**.

3) This **challenged** the **American Dream** (see p.2) at a time when people were already starting to question it. The novel reflected **society's concerns**, so it became very **influential**.

4) The novel captures the '**Jazz Age**' of the 1920s so clearly that the **novel** and the **era** are **inseparable** for most people.

Fitzgerald's Writing Career lasted for 20 years

- **September 1896** — **Born** in **Saint Paul, Minnesota**.
- **1913** — Goes to **Princeton University**.
- **November 1917** — **Leaves Princeton** to **enlist** in the **army**.
- **July 1918** — Meets **Zelda Sayre**, a wealthy socialite.
- **November 1918** — **WWI ends** without Fitzgerald seeing **active duty**.
- **February 1919** — Fitzgerald is **discharged** from the army and gets **engaged** to **Zelda**.
- **June 1919** — Zelda **breaks off** the **engagement**.
- **1920** — His **first book** *This Side of Paradise* is published in March. Zelda and Fitzgerald get **married** in April.
- **October 1921** — Zelda **gives birth** to a **daughter**, **Frances Scott "Scottie"**.
- **April 1925** — *The Great Gatsby* is **published**.
- **1925 - 1940** — Fitzgerald **continues** to write **short stories** and **novels**.
- **December 1940** — **Dies** aged 44.

1896 - 1940

Fitzgerald Drew Heavily on his Own Experiences

Upbringing

Fitzgerald was born into an **upper-middle-class** family, but his father's failure in business made their social position **precarious**. Fitzgerald compared his father to the wealthy men around him, which made him **both admire** and **resent** the **rich**. → Nick's **upper-middle-class** but, like Fitzgerald, Nick has to make his own living. He's **attracted** by the lifestyle of his rich neighbours but **appalled** too.

Relationships

Fitzgerald fell in **love** with **Zelda**, but she **refused** to **marry him** until he could **comfortably support** her. → Gatsby falls in **love** with **Daisy**, a **materialistic** girl who marries a **rich man** instead.

Lifestyle

Fitzgerald lived in **Great Neck**, the **inspiration** for **West Egg**, from 1922 to 1924. He **compromised** his **artistic integrity** by writing **short stories** to fund the **luxurious** life Zelda wanted. → Gatsby **compromises** his **integrity** by bootlegging, in order to get enough money to please Daisy. His **wild parties** echo the Fitzgeralds' **hedonistic** lifestyle.

Historical Background

'The Great Gatsby' was *Written* during the *Jazz Age*

1) *The Great Gatsby* was **published** in **1925** and was set in the '**Roaring Twenties**'. This was a **glamorous** decade marked by **cultural**, **artistic** and **social developments**, but it was brought to an **end** by the **Wall Street Crash** of **1929**, which triggered the **Great Depression** of the 1930s.

2) In the 1920s, **America** became very **prosperous** as the country recovered from **World War I**.

3) There was a **policy** of **Prohibition**. This meant that **alcohol** was **illegal**, but the **continued demand** meant there was a **lot of money** to be made from **bootlegging** (illegally making, supplying or selling alcohol).

4) It was a **time** of great **social change** — the **younger generation** started to **rebel** against **tradition**:

- For many people, and particularly **women**, the **war** provided **new experiences** and **freedom**. **After** the war, there was a strong desire to try **new** and **exciting** things and to **break** from **tradition**. **Jazz** music became **popular** because it was more **energetic** than earlier music styles. Fitzgerald **coined** the term the '**Jazz Age**'.
- **Flappers** began to **challenge traditional gender roles**. Flappers were **women** who **behaved** in a way that was thought to be **inappropriate** by the **older generation** — they **drank**, **smoked** and **wore revealing clothes**.

The *Novel Focuses* on the *American Dream*

1) The **American Dream** is the **idea** that America is a '**land of opportunity**', where a **determined** and **able individual** can **achieve anything**, **regardless** of their **social background**.

2) After the **war** many people, including Fitzgerald, began to **challenge** this **idea** and wonder if it was really **possible**.

3) Fitzgerald was part of a **group of authors** who thought the American Dream had been reduced to the **pursuit of wealth**. They wrote about their **concerns** about the **widespread materialism** of the 1920s.

4) Fitzgerald thought that people who grew up during the war emerged to find "**all Gods dead, all wars fought, all faiths in man shaken**".

'The Great Gatsby' is *Set* in a *Fictional Version* of *Long Island*

1) Fitzgerald sets *The Great Gatsby* in an **altered** version of **Long Island** and **Manhattan**. Great Neck and Manhasset Neck become **East** and **West Eggs**, and the large landfill site at Flushing is renamed the '**valley of ashes**'.

2) The main sites **represent different elements** of the 1920s east-American **lifestyle**:

Manhattan's **skyscrapers** and **luxurious hotel suites** symbolise **wealth**. But it's also filled with **lonely clerks** who spend all their time **working**, and **gangsters** who meet in **seedy bars**.

The **valley of ashes** is a stretch of **wasteland** which sits between the other sites and **connects** them. The valley illustrates that the **excesses** of **wealth** can't be achieved without **exploiting** another part of **society**.

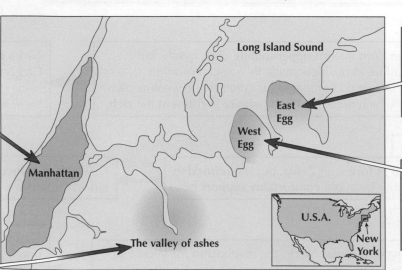

The **wealthy upper classes** who **inherited** their money live in **East Egg**.

West Egg hosts '**new money**' — people who have **earned** their money.

Who's Who in 'The Great Gatsby'

The West Eggers

Affair

The New Yorkers

Relationship

Jay Gatsby...
...is a wealthy and mysterious man who holds lavish parties. He was involved with Daisy and is still in love with her.

Nick Carraway...
...is the narrator of the story. He's just moved to West Egg and lives next door to Gatsby. He's also Daisy's cousin.

Jordan Baker...
...is Nick's love interest and Daisy's best friend. She's a professional golfer who's bored, cynical and independent.

The East Eggers

Affair

Daisy Buchanan...
...is unhappily married to Tom. She was involved with Gatsby but broke it off when she met Tom.

Pammy...
...is their daughter.

Tom Buchanan...
...is married to Daisy and went to university with Nick. He's violent, prejudiced and has lots of affairs.

Meyer Wolfshiem...
...is a well known gambler who's involved in various criminal activities. He's Gatsby's friend and business partner.

The Wastelanders

George Wilson...
...is married to Myrtle, but is initially unaware that she's having an affair. He owns and runs a garage between the Eggs and New York.

Myrtle Wilson...
...is married to George and is Tom's latest mistress. She resents George for being working class and poor.

Catherine...
...is Myrtle's sister. She spends time with Myrtle and Tom when they go to New York.

Other Characters

Dan Cody...
...is a millionaire who mentored Gatsby.

Michaelis...
...runs a café next to Wilson's garage.

Klipspringer & Owl Eyes
...are frequent party-goers at Gatsby's mansion.

Henry Gatz...
...is Gatsby's father.

The McKees...
...are Myrtle's friends in New York.

Novel Synopsis

'The Great Gatsby'... what happens when?

Here's a little recap of the <u>main events</u> in *The Great Gatsby*. It isn't a particularly long novel, but it's hard to remember what happens when, so here's a handy guide to help you work out roughly where to flick to. No need to thank us... unless you really want to.

Chapters 1 and 2 — Nick Moves to West Egg

> Gatsby's **dream** is introduced in Chapter 1, as he reaches out towards the **green light**.

© FAMOUS PLAYERS / LASKY / THE KOBAL COLLECTION

- Nick **claims** that he's **tolerant** and **non-judgemental**.
- Nick's from an **established Midwest family** and has just **moved** to **West Egg** on Long Island to start a **career** in bonds. He rents a bungalow **next door** to a **mansion** owned by a **man** called **Gatsby**.
- Soon after his arrival he goes to **dinner** in **East Egg** at Tom and Daisy Buchanan's mansion. **Daisy** is Nick's **cousin** and he knows **Tom** from **Yale**.
- At their house Nick **meets Jordan Baker**, a **professional golfer**. Tom reveals that he has **strong racial prejudices**.
- During dinner the **phone rings**. Tom goes to answer it and Daisy follows. Jordan tells Nick that it's **Tom's mistress.**
- Daisy tells **Nick** that she **plans** to **set him up** with **Jordan**.
- When Nick goes **home** he **sees Gatsby** reaching out to a **distant green light** across the Sound.
- One afternoon Tom and Nick take the train to **New York**. Tom **introduces** Nick to his **mistress**, **Myrtle**, and her **husband**, **George**. George runs an unsuccessful **garage** in the **wasteland** between New York and the Eggs.
- Nick, Tom and Myrtle go to Tom's **New York apartment** and Myrtle throws an **impromptu party**. Nick **meets** the **McKees** and **Catherine**, Myrtle's sister. They all get **drunk**.
- Myrtle starts **talking about Daisy** — Tom gets **upset** and **breaks her nose**. Nick can only **remember fragments** from the rest of the **night**.

Chapters 3 and 4 — Gatsby is Desperate to See Daisy

> Gatsby's **obsession** with Daisy is revealed in Chapter 4.

- Nick's **invited** to one of Gatsby's **famous parties**.
- At the party he bumps into **Jordan** and hears lots of **wild rumours** about Gatsby's **past**.
- Nick and Jordan **look for** Gatsby and Nick eventually meets him.
- Gatsby talks **privately** with Jordan.
- **After** the party Nick and Jordan start spending time **together**.
- Gatsby **invites Nick** to **lunch** in **New York**. On the way Gatsby tells Nick **unbelievable stories** about his **past**, then says that he needs a **favour** and that Jordan will **explain more**.
- At lunch Gatsby **introduces** Nick to **Meyer Wolfshiem**. Nick introduces Gatsby to **Tom**, but then Gatsby **disappears**.

© ITV/Rex Features

- Nick meets Jordan for tea. She **explains** that Gatsby and Daisy used to be **in love**, but that Daisy **married Tom** whilst Gatsby was away after the **war**. Gatsby wants **Nick** to **arrange** a meeting between him and Daisy.
- Nick and Jordan start having a **relationship**.

Chapters 5 and 6 — Gatsby and Daisy are Reunited

> Gatsby **succeeds** in his **dream** of rekindling his **relationship** with Daisy.

- Nick **invites Gatsby** and **Daisy** to **tea**. Gatsby seems **nervous**, and the **meeting** between him and Daisy is **awkward**.
- Nick **leaves** Gatsby and Daisy **alone together**. When he **returns** they've **restarted** their **relationship**.
- Gatsby gives Nick and Daisy a **tour** of his **mansion** and shows them his **expensive possessions**. Nick leaves them **alone again**.
- Nick reveals Gatsby's **past** to the reader — he used to be **James Gatz**, a farm boy from North Dakota, but he **reinvented** himself as **Jay Gatsby**. He travelled with **Dan Cody**, a **self-made millionaire**, who showed him how to live the **high life**.
- Tom **visits** Gatsby with friends and is **annoyed** to find out that Gatsby **knows Daisy**. Tom **reveals** his **sexist views**.

- Tom and Daisy go to one of Gatsby's **parties**, but Daisy is **disgusted** by it. Gatsby tells Nick that he wants to **re-create** the **past** and make things with Daisy just the **same** as they were **before** she **married Tom**.

Chapters 7 to 9 — Everything Goes Wrong

> Just as Gatsby thinks he's **achieved** his **dream**, it's **shattered** by Tom.

- Gatsby **decides** to **stop** having parties because of Daisy's **reaction** to them. Their **affair continues** and Gatsby **fires** all his **servants** to **prevent** any **gossip**.
- The **Buchanans** invite Jordan, Nick and Gatsby to **lunch**. Tom **realises** that Daisy's having an **affair** with **Gatsby**.
- They **all** go to **New York**, and Tom **stops** for **gas** at **Wilson's garage**. George **tells** Tom that he and Myrtle are **moving away**.
- In New York, Tom aggressively **questions Gatsby** about his **past** and his **relationship** with Daisy. He **accuses Gatsby** of being a **criminal**. Gatsby **claims** that Daisy **never loved Tom**.
- Daisy **decides** that she'd **rather stay** with Tom than **be with Gatsby**. **Knowing** that he's **won**, Tom tells Gatsby and Daisy to **drive home together**.

- On the way **home** Gatsby's car **accidentally hits** and **kills Myrtle**. Tom **blames Gatsby** for Myrtle's **death**.
- Gatsby **tells** Nick that Daisy was **driving** the car that **killed Myrtle**, but that he **plans** to take the **blame**.
- Nick goes to see Gatsby the **following morning** and Gatsby tells Nick the **truth** about his **past**. Nick **reluctantly** goes to **work**. He receives a call from **Jordan** but makes excuses to avoid seeing her.
- When Nick **returns home** he discovers that **George** has **shot Gatsby** and then **killed himself**. Nick tries to **organise** a **big funeral** for Gatsby but **hardly anyone comes**.
- Nick decides to **move back** to the **Midwest**. He **ends** his **relationship** with Jordan and she **accuses** him of being **careless** and **dishonest**. Nick bumps into Tom who **admits** that he **told George** that Gatsby had **killed Myrtle**.
- Nick thinks about the **green light** Gatsby was **reaching towards** when he **first saw him**. He **reflects** that **dreams** of a **better future** can never be **fulfilled** because people can **never escape** their **past**.

'The Great Gatsby' — one of the greatest American novels...

The question of who Gatsby really is will never be answered... but we've tried our darned best to find out. And then we wrote it down in this book. Lucky, lucky you. This book is jammed full of stuff — famous quotations, thematic concerns and character analysis. Plus there's a cartoon at the back of the book...

Chapter One

There are only nine chapters in the novel, but each one's an action-packed mini roller coaster. Seriously. Off we gooo...

Nick Moves to West Egg...

East and West Egg are based on areas of Long Island, near New York, called Great Neck and Manhasset Neck.

- **Nick Carraway** introduces himself as the **narrator**.
- He's just moved to **West Egg**, a **"commuting town"** near **New York**, to start a **career** in **bonds** (finance).
- He goes to **dinner** in **East Egg** with the **Buchanans** — his cousin **Daisy** and her husband **Tom**. At dinner he meets **Jordan Baker** — a **professional golfer**.
- Tom is revealed to be a **racist**. He's also having an **affair** with an **unnamed woman**.
- Nick **returns home** and sees **Gatsby** next door, reaching out across the water towards a **green light**.

Fitzgerald uses this chapter to **set the scene** of the novel:

1) It's made clear that the **events** in the novel have **already** taken place — the characters' **fates** are **already decided**.

2) Most of the **main characters** are **introduced**. Even **Myrtle** is present in a way — her phone call interrupts dinner.

3) Nick talks about **"Midas and Morgan and Maecenas"** — all three men were renowned for their incredible **wealth**. **Morgan** and **Maecenas** were **real men**, whereas **Midas's** story is a **Greek myth** (see p.36). By mentioning both **mythical** and **real** people in the first chapter, Fitzgerald hints that **myth** and **reality** will be **mixed** throughout the book.

... and Explains that he's very Tolerant

There's more detailed analysis of Nick as a narrator on pages 46-47

1) Nick claims that he **remembers** his **father's advice** when he **meets new people** — other people haven't had the **"advantages that [he's] had"**. This gives the impression that he's **tolerant**, and has strong **moral** and **family** values.

2) However, Nick admits that he repeats his father's advice **"snobbishly"**, and the fact that his father had to tell him not to **judge people** too **harshly** suggests that this is one of Nick's **failings**. Nick's claim that he has a better **"sense of the fundamental decencies"** than most people also makes him seem **judgemental**. This mix of **self-awareness** and **arrogance** is typical of the **complex contradictions** in **Nick's character**.

3) There are **hints** that Nick can be **intolerant** and **judgemental**, e.g. he says that he **"feigned sleep"** when people confided in him, he views Gatsby's life with **"unaffected scorn"**, and he's **"disgusted"** by Tom and Daisy's marriage. This makes the reader less **trusting** of his narration because it suggests that he's **dishonest**.

4) Nick sometimes **misreads** situations, which also makes his narration **untrustworthy**. He thinks Daisy has **everything** she **wants** so he sees in her eyes **"the absence of all desire"**. But we later find out that she has **"had a very bad time"**.

Geography and Morality are Linked

1) Fitzgerald uses the **superficial similarities** between the **Eggs** to emphasise how **different** they **really** are — they're **"identical in contour"**, but dissimilar **"in every particular except shape and size"**.

2) He also gives each **location** a **different morality**, which encourages the reader to make **comparisons** between them:

The **MIDWEST** is...	• **Old fashioned** and represents **family values** — the Carraways are a **"prominent, well-to-do"** **"clan"**, and **Nick's father** runs the **same hardware business** that his **Great Uncle** set up.
	• Possibly **dishonest** under the surface — the **"founder"** of Nick's family **avoided** the Civil War by sending a **"substitute"** and they all **pretend** that they're **"descended from the Dukes of Buccleuch"**.
EAST EGG is...	• **Conservative** and **aristocratic** but not as **refined** as it **appears**. E.g. Tom is **"aggressive"** and **"hulking"**, where typically the **upper classes** should be **polite** and **well-mannered**.
	• **Fashionable** but **fake**. Its **appealing surface** hides **unattractive realities** — the Buchanans' marriage isn't as **happy** as it seems, and **Daisy's** looks and **wealth** mask a **bored, cynical** and **empty interior**.
WEST EGG is...	• **Home** to the **new rich** who've made their **own fortunes** rather than **inheriting** money — most of the **residents** don't have **aristocratic breeding** or wealthy **family connections** (but **Nick's** an **exception**).
	• **Characterised** by **extravagant displays** of **wealth** that are in **poor taste**, e.g. Gatsby's mansion.

3) **New York**, the **fourth location**, also has a **distinct moral character** — this is **explored** in **Chapter 2** (see p.8).

Chapter One

Dinner conversation *Highlights Prejudices*

Nick **visits** the **Buchanans'** for **dinner** — everything **appears civilised** and **carefree** at **first**, but **tensions** and **prejudices** soon **start** to **emerge**:

This is an allusion to a real book called 'The Rising Tide of Color Against White World-Supremacy' which argued that white people were at threat from other races.

Racism

1) Tom tries to explain how **science** has "**proved**" that **white people** are "**the dominant race**", but they're **under threat**. He tells Nick about a "**fine book**" called "*The Rise of the Coloured Empires*".

2) **Fitzgerald** is **highlighting** the **fear** of **immigration** in **America in the 1920s**. However, it's clear that Fitzgerald is **mocking racism**. Tom is incoherent and "**full of hesitation**" — the reader isn't supposed to **empathise** with him.

Sexism

1) In some ways, Daisy and Jordan seem **independent** and **satisfied**. Their eyes are "**free from all desire**", and Nick portrays them as being in **control** of the **social gathering** — "**they accepted Tom and me**". But ultimately, the society in *The Great Gatsby* is very **sexist**.

2) For example, Tom suggests **Jordan's freedom** should be **restricted**: "**they oughtn't to let her run around the country in this way**".

3) Daisy **believes** that her **society** doesn't **value intelligence** in **women**, which is why she hoped her daughter would be "**a beautiful little fool**".

4) Her comment hints that, although she **ignores** Tom's **infidelities**, she's **upset** by them. She believes she'd be **happier** if she was a "**fool**" who didn't **realise** he was cheating.

5) Daisy has **some control** over Tom — she shakes "**her head decisively**" and won't let him **answer** the second call. But she still **has** to pretend with "**tense gaiety**" that everything is fine and put a **brave face** on her **humiliation**.

© United Archives GmbH / Alamy

Nick gets a *Glimpse* of Gatsby's Deep Longing

1) The chapter **ends** with Nick's **first sight** of Gatsby — a **lonely figure** reaching out towards a "**single green light**". Nick **doesn't know** what the light **represents** to Gatsby, which creates **mystery**.

2) Gatsby's **obsessive focus** on this distant **point** is **striking**. He's so **desperate** with longing that he's "**trembling**".

3) The **first thing** we learn about Gatsby is his **powerful desire** for a **mysterious aim** — this suggests that this is the **most important aspect** of his **character**. In **contrast**, the East Eggers have an obvious **lack** of **motivation** or **drive**.

4) Fitzgerald uses **light** to **symbolise dreams** and **desires** — the green light **represents** Gatsby's **dream** of being with Daisy — and his "**stretched out**" arms show that he's still **striving to achieve it**. In contrast, Daisy's **attitude** towards the **candles** as she "**snapped them out**" could symbolise that she's **given up** on her dreams.

5) **Light** is also **used** to **set the scene**:

- When conversation is **friendly**, the light is **soft** and "**rosy-coloured**" — this makes it seem **warm** and **happy**.
- When Tom's **mistress phones** "**the glow faded**". This **suggests** that things **aren't** as **happy** as they **seem**.
- The **shift** from **natural** to **artificial light** as they move inside reflects the fact that Nick's **romantic views** of Tom and Daisy's life have been **shattered**.

Practice Questions

Q1 'Even though Nick claims he's not judgemental, his presentation of the other characters encourages the reader to make their own judgements about them.' To what extent do you agree with this statement? Refer to the text in your answer.

Q2 Using Chapter 1 as a starting point, analyse the importance and the role of light and colour in enhancing the different themes and moods of the novel. Give examples from the text in your answer.

"I've had a very bad time, Nick, and I'm pretty cynical about everything"

What a cheery beginning — nobody seems very happy except for Nick, and that's mainly because he's only just arrived. Imagine how depressed he'll be when he realises the Bonds business isn't all about cars, women, and martinis — shaken not stirred...

Chapter Two

Start spreading the news, I'm leaving today, I want to be a part of it — New York, New York!

Nick, Tom *and* Tom's Mistress Head *to* New York...

© akg-images / Album / Paramount Pictures

- **Nick** meets Tom's mistress **Myrtle** and her husband, **George**. They own a **garage** on the edge of the **valley of ashes** between West Egg and New York.

- Myrtle **agrees** to go to **New York** with Nick and Tom.

- Myrtle hosts an **impromptu party** in Tom's New York **apartment**. She invites her **sister** and the **McKees**, who live in the **apartment below**.

- They all get **drunk**. Tom and Myrtle **argue** and he **breaks** her **nose**.

1) Nick tries to **distance** himself from the others and narrate as an **observational bystander** rather than a **participant** in their **immoral lifestyle**. He doesn't explicitly give his **opinion**, which suggests he wants to sound **objective**.

2) But his **language** shows that he **judges** them **harshly**. He thinks Tom is "**supercilious**" and Mrs McKee is "**shrill**".

3) He tries to **maintain** the **moral high ground**, claiming that he only meets Myrtle because Tom "**literally forced**" him.

4) But Nick also admits to being both "**enchanted and repelled**" by the situation — he feels "**entangled**" and can't leave.

Two *New Settings are* Introduced

The "valley of ashes" could be a reference to T.S. Eliot's 'The Waste Land', published three years previously (see p.48).

1) The "**valley of ashes**" is a place of **poverty** that is used as a **dumping ground** for all the **waste** produced by the city — it's the **ugly by-product** of **consumerism** that is forgotten by the **wealthy Egg communities**.

2) Its **bleak** and **barren** nature provides a **contrast** to the **loudness** and **brightness** of New York and the **beautiful exterior** of the two Eggs — but also **symbolises** the **moral decay** and **ugliness** hidden **underneath** their surfaces. **T.J Eckleburg's advertisement** looks out **indifferently** at the **desolation** (see pages 40 and 42).

3) The upper classes try to **ignore** the **reality** of the valley. E.g. Nick imagines that there are "**romantic apartments concealed overhead**", but actually the entire garage is "**unprosperous and bare**".

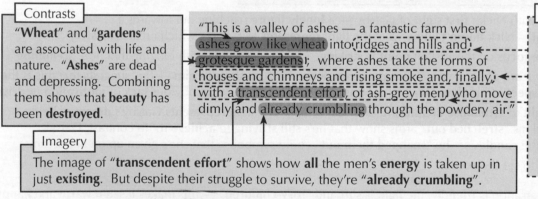

Contrasts

"**Wheat**" and "**gardens**" are associated with life and nature. "**Ashes**" are dead and depressing. Combining them shows that **beauty** has been **destroyed**.

"This is a valley of ashes — a fantastic farm where ashes grow like wheat into ridges and hills and grotesque gardens; where ashes take the forms of houses and chimneys and rising smoke and, finally, with a transcendent effort, of ash-grey men who move dimly and already crumbling through the powdery air."

Lists

Fitzgerald gives **long lists** of the objects made from ash to **emphasise** the scale of **decay**. Repetition of "**and**" slows the pace, emphasising the **trudging drudgery** of life in the valley.

Imagery

The image of "**transcendent effort**" shows how **all** the men's **energy** is taken up in just **existing**. But despite their struggle to survive, they're "**already crumbling**".

4) **New York represents wild**, **selfish behaviour** and the **pursuit of pleasure**. This is illustrated by the fact that it's the **setting** for Tom and Myrtle's **affair**. The **drunken debauchery** of Myrtle's party demonstrates the city's lack of **moral depth** — people feel they can **act** how they **want** without **fear** of the **consequences**.

Myrtle *Only Cares* about Appearances *and* Material Possessions

1) Myrtle claims not to care about **clothes** — "**I just slip it on sometimes when I don't care what I look like**", but actually she's **obsessed** with her **appearance** — she **changes clothes** regularly and buys **cold cream** and **perfume**.

2) She wears **bold colours**, in **contrast** to **Daisy** who wears **white**. But when Myrtle changes into a **cream** dress, her "**vitality**" changes to "**hauteur**" (arrogance). This shows that she thinks **breeding** is all about **appearances**.

3) She's also concerned with **other people's appearances**. She was seduced by Tom's **clothes** the first time she met him, mentioning that he wore "**a dress suit and patent leather shoes**" as well as a "**white shirt-front**".

4) It's **significant** that Myrtle pretended to be "**looking at the advertisement**" instead of looking at Tom, because both Tom and the advertised product represent Myrtle's greed for **material objects** and **wealth**.

Chapter Two

There are a lot of Unhappy Marriages

For more on love and relationships see p.38.

There are only **three** marriages **specifically mentioned** in *The Great Gatsby* and none of them seem very **happy**:

BUCHANANS
- Myrtle's **description** of how she met Tom suggests that he has had **many affairs**. She says "**he knew I lied**" — this shows he's **confident** and **practiced** in his **seduction**.
- **Catherine** says Daisy **refuses** to divorce Tom because she's "**a Catholic**", but Nick knows she **isn't**. This implies that Tom has **lied** to Myrtle to hide the fact that he doesn't want to **leave** Daisy.
- He **refuses** to allow Myrtle to even **say** Daisy's name and **breaks** her **nose** when she starts shouting it. This suggests Tom has strong feelings of **possessiveness** towards Daisy.

WILSONS
- Myrtle **resents** and **despises** Wilson. When he's mentioned, her response is "**violent and obscene**".
- She thinks he's **beneath** her **socially**, and claims that "**he wasn't fit to lick my shoe**".
- She **won't accept** that it was **her choice** to **marry** him, saying she **mistook** him for a "**gentleman**".

MCKEES
- Mr McKee has **photographed** his wife "**a hundred and twenty-seven times**", which could suggest that he's obsessed with her as a **visual object**, rather than as an **individual**.
- Their **lack** of **communication** reinforces this — he ignores Mrs McKee for most of the **party**, **shushing her** at one point and **only acknowledging her** by nodding "**in a bored way**".

All three marriages seem to be more about appearances than love.

The Working Classes are treated Badly

1) Tom is rough with **both** Daisy and Myrtle, but where Daisy's **bruised knuckle** is an **accident**, Myrtle's **bloody**, **broken nose** is **deliberate**. It's **easy** for Tom to **violently injure** Myrtle — it's just a "**short deft movement**". This suggests that the **working classes** are **vulnerable** to the **whims** of the **upper classes**.

2) Tom's also **cruel** to **Wilson** — he raises his hopes by **promising** to **sell him a car**, but keeps **putting it off** until "**next week**". This gives Tom **power** over Wilson.

3) Nick's descriptions of Myrtle are **mocking** and **unsympathetic**. He says she has a "**mincing shout**", becomes "**violently affected**" and "**flounced**" around her flat. His **critical tone** suggests that he **judges** her for **pretending** to be **upper class**.

Alcohol is a Negative Influence

Fitzgerald's negative portrayal of alcohol affects the reader's reaction to Gatsby later in the novel. The fact that he's a bootlegger links him to the corrupting influence of alcohol.

Alcohol seems to be a part of life in **New York**. Fitzgerald shows that it has **negative effects** on the people who **abuse it**:

1) **Nick** describes Tom as having "**tanked up**" and then claims that Tom's behaviour "**bordered on violence**". After **more drinks**, Tom breaks Myrtle's nose — this clearly **links alcohol** and **violence**.
2) Alcohol **lowers inhibitions** — after drinking whisky, Myrtle sits on "**Tom's lap**" with **no discretion**.
3) Nick's **narration** is **confused** and **fragmented** because the alcohol has affected his **memory** of events. This contrasts with his usual **narrative style** and highlights the **loss** of **control** caused by alcohol.

Practice Questions

Q1 'Myrtle Wilson cares more about appearances than any other character in the novel.' To what extent do you agree with this statement? Back up your answer with examples from the text.

Q2 Using Chapter 2 as a starting point, analyse the role of marriage in *The Great Gatsby* and assess whether any of the romantic relationships in the novel can be considered a success. Refer to the text in your answer.

"Neither of them can stand the person they're married to"

Unlike Tom and Myrtle, I adore the person I'm married to. They're always there for me, they provide me with all the tea and biscuits I need, and best of all they give me a pile of money every month. I should probably clarify that I'm married to my job.

Chapter Three

Nick finally meets the eponymous hero of his story, but he doesn't even realise...

An eponymous character is the title character of the work e.g. Gatsby in *The Great Gatsby.*

Nick Goes *to one of* Gatsby's Parties...

- **Nick receives** an **invitation** to one of Gatsby's **famous parties** and visits his neighbour's **mansion** for the **first time**.
- Nick spends the **evening** with **Jordan Baker** trying to **find** the **host** of the party, **Jay Gatsby**, but they just hear a lot of **wild gossip** and **rumours**. When Nick **finally meets** Gatsby he's **nothing like** what he **expected**.
- Gatsby **speaks** to Jordan about a **private matter** but Jordan **refuses** to **tell Nick** what Gatsby said.
- **After** the party Nick gives a **brief description** of his **life in New York** and his **developing relationship** with Jordan.

1) The **poetic language** lends a **magical atmosphere** to the **parties**. Gatsby's **"blue gardens"** are alive with **"the whisperings and the champagne and the stars"** — the **list form** draws together **sound**, **taste** and **sight**.

2) The party scene seems to **increase** in **pace** as the **evening progresses**, and Nick's **perspective changes** as well — **initially** Nick sees everything from **far away** and it seems **romantic** and **poetic**: **"floating rounds of cocktails permeate the garden outside, until the air is alive with chatter and laughter"**.

3) Later, when Nick **focuses** in on **people** and **becomes involved** in the **party's action**, everything becomes **sharp** and **vivid**: **"She narrowed her eyes and shivered. Lucille shivered. We all turned and looked around for Gatsby"**.

4) The **wild excess** and **drunkenness** at Gatsby's **parties** suggest that Fitzgerald wanted to give a sense of both the **depravity** and the **hedonism** of the **wealthy** in **1920s America**. There's a **sharp contrast** between the guests' **bad behaviour** and the **magical surroundings**. This **highlights** both Nick and Fitzgerald's **simultaneous attraction** and **repulsion** for the **era**.

The emptiness of this lifestyle is symbolised by the "oranges and lemons" that are reduced to "pulpless halves" by Monday.

Owl Eyes *is an* Unusual Guest

1) Nick meets a **"stout, middle-aged man, with enormous owl-eyed spectacles"** in Gatsby's library. This man, later known as **'Owl Eyes'**, is amazed that Gatsby's **books** are **"real"**. Fitzgerald uses Owl Eyes to highlight the **tension** between **appearance** and **reality** in Gatsby's life. The books are **real** but have **never been read** — they're **props**.

2) Owl Eyes emphasises the importance of **appearance** in the Egg Community. He **praises** Gatsby's attention to detail in **maintaining** the **illusion** that he's a **well-read gentleman**. He compares Gatsby to **David Belasco**, a **Broadway producer** known for his **realistic sets**, as if Gatsby's an **entertainer** or **illusionist**.

3) Owl Eyes himself could be a **symbolic presence** in the library. **Owls** are traditionally seen as **symbols** of **wisdom** and Owl Eyes is the **only guest** to see through Gatsby's persona. However, owls are also seen as **bad omens**:

> ### Foreshadowing
>
> - Owl Eyes mutters to himself that **"if one brick was removed the whole library was liable to collapse"**. Fitzgerald is using Owl Eyes to emphasise the point that if **one part** of Gatsby's **outward image** were to **falter**, the **entire illusion** would be **shattered**. This foreshadows the way that Gatsby's life will **fall apart**.
> - Owl Eyes is involved in a **car crash** as he leaves the party. He's **mistakenly thought** to be the **driver** — **"You don't understand... I wasn't driving"**. This **foreshadows** Gatsby's involvement in Myrtle's **death**.

The *Mysterious* Gatsby *is Revealed*

1) The **rumours** surrounding Gatsby **continue** — Gatsby is said to have **"killed a man"** and to have been **"a German spy"**.

2) Jordan says he **"was an Oxford man"** and Nick starts to imagine a **"dim background"**, but when she says that she **doesn't believe it**, the **mystery** starts **building again**. All that Jordan really knows is that **"he gives large parties"**.

3) When Nick meets Gatsby, he pays close attention to Gatsby's **smile** which has **"a quality of eternal reassurance"**. Nick **describes** the smile using words like **"believe"**, **"impression"** and **"convey"**, and comments on Gatsby's affected **"formality of speech"** — this gives an **early hint** that Gatsby's **smile** and **speech** are part of a **deliberately crafted persona** (see p.24).

Chapter Three

Underneath the *Glamour*, *Gatsby's party is full of* **Bad Behaviour**

1) **Despite** the fact that the East Egg 'old rich' deny the West Egg 'new rich' entry to the American 'upper class', both communities **attend** Gatsby's parties. The **East Egg community** are "**carefully on guard**" to **maintain** their **respectability**. However, in reality the **East Eggers** arc just as **badly behaved** as the **West Eggers**.

2) There are suggestions of **sexual promiscuity** amongst the guests — one East Egg woman tries to stop her husband from **flirting** by hissing "**You promised!**" into his ear, which **implies** that her husband often **behaves badly**.

3) The **Englishmen** are desperate to **follow** the **American Dream**. They talk business, even at the party: "**looking a little hungry, and all talking in low, earnest voices**". Their '**hunger**' for wealth is **always present**.

Gatsby and Nick are **Both Isolated**

1) Gatsby's party is **packed** — he seems to be a **popular man**. But **most of the time** he **lives alone** in an **empty house**:

   - Gatsby stands "**alone**" at the edge of his party. The wilder the party gets, the more Gatsby seems like an **outsider** — he doesn't **drink**, he doesn't **flirt** and he grows "**more correct as the fraternal hilarity increased**".

   - At the end of the party, when the "**laughter and sound**" has died away, Gatsby is shown in "**complete isolation**" with his "**hand up in formal gesture of farewell**". The image of the lonely figure **echoes** the end of Chapter 1, where Gatsby "**stretched out his arms toward the dark water**", reaching out for Daisy.

2) Nick **doesn't belong** in either the **Egg community** or in **New York**.

   - Nick emphasises that he was "**invited**" to Gatsby's **party**, whereas others just **turned up**. Nick feels **morally superior** to the others — he **ends** the chapter by claiming that he's "**one of the few honest people**" he's met.

   - Nick describes Gatsby's party as "**spectroscopic**". 'Spectroscopy' is the **study** of **light** and **colour**, so Fitzgerald's use of the **word** suggests that the party is **full of bright lights** and colourful outfits. However, Nick is dressed in **white**, which makes him **stand out** from the crowd.

   - Nick seems **uncomfortable** in **company** — other people easily **engage** in "**enthusiastic meetings**" **despite** the fact that they "**never knew each other's names**", whereas Nick feels "**purposeless and alone**".

   - In **New York** Nick suffers from a "**haunting loneliness**". He **imagines** entering the lives of "**romantic women**" but **never acts** on his **desires**. There's a **contrast** between Nick's **dinner**, the "**gloomiest event**" of his day, and the "**gaiety**" and "**intimate excitement**" of others — Nick wants to be **involved** but remains an **outsider**.

Jordan Baker is **Developed** *as a* **Love Interest** *for* **Nick**

1) Nick's **interest** in **Jordan** seems to come from his **fascination** with the fact that she "**concealed something**" from the **world**. Like Gatsby, Jordan has **developed** a set of "**affectations**" to allow her to feel "**safer**" and **more confident**.

2) Nick claims that Jordan "**deliberately shifted our relations**" so that he's made to **think** that he "**loved her**". This suggests that Jordan is **in control** of the relationship and is able to **manipulate** Nick.

3) Nick **recognises** that Jordan's "**incurably dishonest**" and "**careless**" and a **part** of the **lifestyle** he holds in **contempt**. Their **relationship** suggests that Nick's **begun** to **embrace** the **hedonism** of Eastern life.

Practice Questions

Q1 Nick describes himself as "honest" but in the final chapter Jordan Baker disagrees. To what extent does Fitzgerald portray Nick as honest? Assess whether the reader is supposed to believe that Nick is "honest".

Q2 'In revealing his hopes, dreams and ambitions to Jordan Baker, Gatsby seals his own fate.' How far do you agree with this statement? Refer to the text in your answer.

"I hate careless people. That's why I like you"

Just like Jordan, I hate carless people. Always wandering around getting in my way when I'm cruising round town in my Porsche. Oh hang on, she said <u>careless</u> people — well that's a completely different thing. Mind you, I don't like them much either...

Chapter Four

Nick goes with Gatsby to New York and they finally have some one-on-one time. A real manly man-to-man chat.

Nick **Learns More** about **Gatsby**, but there are still **Mysteries** to **Uncover**...

- **Nick** makes a **list** of some of the **people** who **attended** Gatsby's **parties** in the **summer** of **1922**.
- **Gatsby invites** Nick to **lunch** in **New York**. Gatsby tells Nick a **story** about his **past**.
- At lunch Nick **meets Meyer Wolfshiem**, a notorious **gambler**.
- Nick **meets Jordan** for **dinner** and she **explains** that Gatsby and Daisy used to be in **love**.

The **structure** of this chapter is in **three** parts:

1) Nick **lists** Gatsby's party guests. Nick **drops names** as if the **reader** should **recognise** them as **celebrities**. He also lists their **misbehaviour** — they're remembered for **gambling**, for "**a fight with a bum**", and **more sinister behaviour** — one guest "**killed himself**" and another "**strangled his wife**". This emphasises the **darkness beneath** the **wealthy**, **carefree** and **lavish lifestyle**.

2) Gatsby takes Nick to lunch with Wolfshiem. It's the **first time** the reader catches a **glimpse** of the **real Gatsby**. His stories are so **outrageous** that they prompt the reader to wonder what he's **hiding**. His **connection** with **Wolfshiem** raises the **suspicion** that Gatsby may be a **criminal**.

3) However, Jordan's **description** of Gatsby's **past romance** with **Daisy** gives a **different impression** of Gatsby — it portrays him as an **innocent**, **romantic young soldier** and shows **another side** to his **personality**. It also adds another **layer of mystery**.

Gatsby's **Past Remains Ambiguous**

1) The chapter opens with "**the world and his mistress**" **casually** sharing **rumours** about Gatsby's **identity**. **Accusations** that he "**killed a man**" are made in between **drinks** from "**that there crystal glass**", indicating that the **relaxed guests** have no **concerns** about their **host's potential corruption**.

2) **Gatsby** tells Nick about his past on the way to **New York**. Nick pays **close attention** to Gatsby's voice and comments that Gatsby "**hurried the phrase**" about attending Oxford, and "**swallowed it**", as if he's **lying**.

3) **Gatsby** shows Nick an "**authentic**" looking **medal**, and a **photo** from **Oxford**, which seem to '**prove**' that his **persona** is not just an **act**. Fitzgerald **encourages** the **reader** to think that Gatsby is **lying**, before suddenly giving **credibility** to Gatsby's story. This means that Gatsby's **past remains** a **mystery**.

4) Gatsby claims he's from the '**Middle West**', but when **questioned** by Nick, **specifies** that he's from **San Francisco**, which is on the **West Coast**, **hundreds** of **miles away** from the **Middle West**. Nick says "**I see**", suggesting that he's **seen through** Gatsby's **persona** — but Fitzgerald leaves it **ambiguous**.

5) Gatsby's **heart to heart** with Nick seems to be **motivated** by the fact that he wants to ask a **favour**. By **apparently confiding** in Nick about his **past**, Gatsby **hopes** to **build rapport** with him.

Gatsby has **Criminal Connections**

1) Nick's **initial description** of New York makes it sound **clean** and **attractive**. It looks like "**sugar lumps**" and was built using "**non-olfactory**" (scentless) **money**. This **idealised description** focuses on the **beauty** of the city, which implies it's **free** of the **stench of corruption**.

2) However, the level of **corruption** is so **great** in New York that even the **police** can be **bribed**. Gatsby manages to **avoid** a speeding fine with a "**white card**" that he can't satisfactorily explain the **significance** of.

3) When they meet **Meyer Wolfshiem**, Gatsby's involvement with the **criminal underworld** is strongly **implied**. They have lunch in the "**half-darkness**" of the cellar, which suggests it's a place of **shady dealings**.

> Gatsby's **association** with Wolfshiem shows **another side** to his **character** — it **implies** that his **lavish lifestyle** is **funded** by **crime**. Gatsby **symbolises** both the **luxury** and the **corruption** of the **Jazz Age**. **Tom Buchanan** is also in the restaurant, which shows that even **established families** and **outwardly respectable** people **ignore** the **prohibition law** — New York's **corruption** has spread throughout society.

Chapter Four

Jordan Reveals Daisy and Gatsby's Past

1) The second part of this chapter **shifts** to Jordan's **first-person narrative**. Nick tells the **story** in **her voice**.

2) Jordan describes Daisy's **early relationship** with Gatsby, and **explains** that a **letter** from **Gatsby** almost **persuaded** Daisy to reject Tom the **night before** their **wedding**.

3) Fitzgerald **contrasts Daisy's behaviour** with **Gatsby's**. While Daisy is **briefly distressed** by Gatsby's letter, she **marries Tom** "**without so much as a shiver**". Gatsby's **constancy** highlights his **loyal** and **romantic nature**.

4) Jordan's story makes Gatsby into a **more sympathetic character**, and for **Nick**, Gatsby becomes a **real person** — he was "**delivered suddenly from the womb of his purposeless splendour**". Nick's **changing opinion** of Gatsby reminds the **reader** that the novel is written from Nick's **point of view**, which **introduces bias**.

5) Her story also suggests that **none** of the **characters** have **changed**:

- Gatsby is **still obsessed** with Daisy and continues to have a "**romantic**" **desire** for her.
- Tom began **cheating early** in his **marriage**, having an **affair** with a **chambermaid**. His **affair** with Myrtle is his latest "**spree**" — he's been **unfaithful** throughout his **marriage**.
- Daisy is **easily led** — Gatsby's **letter** makes her **decide** not to **marry Tom**, but she's quickly **persuaded** to **go ahead** with the **wedding**.

Gatsby's Dream is a Corruption of the American Dream

1) As Nick and Jordan drive through Central Park they overhear a **popular Jazz song** about "**The Sheik of Araby**":

In this song the Sheik has a '**captured bride**' and conquers '**love by fear**' — the song seems to **satirise** the situation **as seen** by **Gatsby**, with the Sheik being a **reference** to **Tom Buchanan**. The song is sung by "**the clear voices of children**", which makes the **violence** of the lyrics all the more **sinister**.

2) The **song's lyrics** suggest that Gatsby sees Daisy as an **unwilling victim** of marriage — this is an **early hint** that he wants to **recapture** his **past** with Daisy, and **pretend** that her marriage **never happened**.

3) Gatsby's **obsession** with **Daisy** can be seen to **symbolise** the **American Dream** (see p.37). The **image** of him as a **lone figure**, reaching out for the **green light** (see p.11) shows him **striving** for the **object** of his **desires**.

© PARAMOUNT / THE KOBAL COLLECTION

4) The fact that Gatsby **strives** to **win Daisy**, who's **shallow**, **snobbish** and **fickle**, **reflects** the **corruption** of the **American Dream** — it has become focused on the **shallow pursuit** of **wealth**.

5) Gatsby also **doesn't care** that **breaking up** Daisy's **marriage** is immoral — he claims it's "**nothing underhand**". The 'American Dream' has become about **individual satisfaction**, not **reaping** the **rewards** of **hard work**.

6) Nick **juxtaposes** the **physical reality** of Jordan, "**the girl beside me**" with the **dream image** of Daisy's "**disembodied face**" to show that the **woman** Gatsby **loves** is just a **dream**. He also **associates** Daisy with the "**blinding signs**" of New York **shops**, which symbolises the way that Gatsby's **dream** of Daisy is **tied up** with his dream of **financial success**.

Practice Questions

Q1 Using the car journey to New York in Chapter 4 as a starting point, assess whether the reader ever gets to see the real Gatsby in the novel. Refer to the text in your answer.

Q2 Looking at the novel as a whole, analyse whether Jordan's description of Gatsby as "regular tough underneath it all" is a fair assessment of his character.

"Anything can happen now that we've slipped over this bridge... anything at all"

Nick points out that in New York, anything goes. It's where all the really immoral stuff happens in the novel. When I went to New York I didn't see anything immoral. Such a disappointment. You'd think the Statue of Liberty would have at least flashed a bit of leg...

Chapter Five

Scandal in West Egg — a man invited a woman to tea. Without her husband. Fetch me my smelling salts quick...

Gatsby and Daisy are Reunited...

- **Nick** and **Gatsby arrange** a **date** to invite **Daisy** for **tea**. Nick **tells her** not to bring **Tom**.
- The **reunion** between Gatsby and Daisy is **awkward** and **uncomfortable** so Nick **leaves** the room. After a while Nick **returns**, and they decide to **visit Gatsby's mansion**.
- After a **brief tour** of the mansion **Nick leaves** Daisy and Gatsby **alone together**.

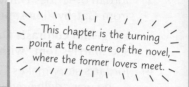

This chapter is the turning point at the centre of the novel, where the former lovers meet.

Chapter 5 uses **imagery** of **light** throughout:

1) At the beginning Gatsby's house is **"blazing with light"**. Nick's describes the scene in a **dramatic tone**, reflecting his fear that his house was **"on fire"**. In contrast, Gatsby's response is casual and distracted: **"I have been glancing into some of the rooms"**. Gatsby is **preoccupied** with the idea of finally **proving** his **worth** to Daisy.

2) The chapter **ends** with another **image** of **electrical lighting**: **"All the lights were going on in West Egg now"**.

3) In the central part of this chapter, the **two reunited lovers** provide a different sort of light — Gatsby **"literally glowed"** and the room fills with **"twinkle-bells of sunshine"**. The **contrast** between **electrical** and 'natural' lighting **emphasises** the lovers' **joy** and **gentle innocence** at this point in the novel.

However, Fitzgerald uses **pathetic fallacy** to suggest that their **reunion** will not have a **happy fate** — it's **marred** by **"pouring rain"** and a **"damp mist"**. It only **rains twice** in the novel, the other time being **Gatsby's funeral**.

Fitzgerald Questions Nick's Morality

1) The chapter **begins** with a **conversation** between Nick and Gatsby, and Gatsby makes Nick a **business proposition**. Nick **turns down** the proposition, which he seems to suspect is **illegal**, but his **main reason** for doing so is that he feels Gatsby is trying to **pay** him for a **"service to be rendered"**. Nick seems to **care less** that the business is probably **illegal** than that Gatsby is only offering it to him out of a **sense of duty**.

> **Nick is a moral character**
>
> The two men are positioned at the **boundary** of their **gardens**, where Gatsby's **neatly mown "expanse"** of grass meets Nick's **"ragged lawn"**. The **pristine** appearance of **Gatsby's garden symbolises** the way his **glossy lifestyle covers up** the less respectable **"little business on the side"**. Nick's **unkempt garden** suggests that he's **less concerned** with **appearances** and is a **more honest** character.

2) However, Nick's sense of **morality** is not **consistent**. In Chapter 1 Nick **explains** that his **tolerance** has a **limit**, but in this chapter it's suggested that his **morality** also has a limit. Nick's **feelings of disgust** for the **hedonistic behaviour** of the **East** have been overcome by his **fascination** with it.

> **Nick is morally corrupt**
>
> In **Chapter 2** he **witnesses** Tom and Myrtle's **affair** even though he **claims** he doesn't want to. In Chapter 5, Nick **helps** Gatsby arrange a **private meeting** with Daisy, which makes him **complicit** in their **affair**. The **misted windows** of Nick's **house** during this meeting could **symbolise** Nick's **inability** to **see** that his **complicity** is **immoral**.

3) Fitzgerald **questions** whether Nick has **become a part** of the **society** he has such **distaste** for.

Gatsby's Stuck in the Past

1) When Gatsby meets Daisy he nearly causes a **clock** to **fall** from the mantelpiece (see p.55). **Significantly**, this clock is already **"defunct"** — **time** has **stopped** for Gatsby because he's **fixated** on the **past**.

2) **Gatsby** seems **determined** to **re-create** himself in the image of a **European aristocrat**. He **imports** his **shirts** from **England**, decorates his house with **"Marie Antoinette music rooms and Restoration Salons"** in the style of **French** and **English royalty**, and has a **replica** of **"the Merton College Library"** at Oxford University.

3) This **corrupts** the **core** of the **American Dream** — instead of wanting to **celebrate** the **determination** of the American **working man**, Gatsby seems to want to be part of the **high society** of the old European **hierarchy**.

Chapter Five

Gatsby and Daisy are presented Sympathetically

In this chapter Fitzgerald dramatically changes the adjectives used to describe Gatsby to create an entirely different image of the character.

1) Gatsby's **adopted persona** begins to **break down** in this chapter. Fitzgerald presents a **sympathetic view** of Gatsby in a **vulnerable position**:

- Gatsby's normally **calm exterior** is replaced with **"suppressed eagerness"**. He's nervous about being left alone with Daisy and tries to stay close to Nick: **"He followed me wildly [...] and whispered 'Oh God!'"**.
- His **carefully considered language** is replaced with an **"automatic quality"**. Even his well-rehearsed phrase **"old sport"** is almost **forgotten**: **"he added hollowly, '... old sport'"**.
- The **reader** is **shown** Gatsby as his party guests **never see** him — the **nervous** and **likeable lovesick fool**.

2) **Daisy** is also **presented** in a **positive light**, and together their **behaviour** and **language** lend the chapter an **innocent tone**.

- Her **voice** becomes **"artificial"** and her **behaviour** becomes **"frightened but graceful"** when she **meets** Gatsby — she's **genuinely shocked** and doesn't know how to **react**. Daisy's **elegant persona** breaks down.
- She's **overwhelmed** with **feelings** — and she cries **"stormily"** which suggests **deep emotions**.
- Her **romantic nature** is also revealed — she admires the **"sparkling"** and **"pale gold odour"** of flowers, and is **enchanted** by the **"pink and golden billow of foamy clouds"**. Her focus on **nature** implies that there's **more** to her than just a **love** of **material possessions**.

However, Nick **tends** to **analyse Gatsby's emotions** and **actions** on a **deep level**, but presents **Daisy's behaviour** in a **shallow, descriptive manner**. For example, he describes Gatsby as having been **"at an inconceivable pitch of intensity"**, whereas Daisy is just **superficially described** as admiring her **surroundings**: **"Daisy took the brush with delight and smoothed her hair"**. In this way Nick **highlights** Daisy's **materialism** compared to Gatsby's **idealism**.

Appearances are Everything

1) **Appearances** mean **everything** to **Daisy**, so Gatsby is **desperate** to **maintain** his **adopted persona**. He tries to **present himself** and his **home** in a **luxurious way** to **appeal** to **Daisy**. He **wears** a **silver shirt** with a **gold tie** to emphasise his wealth, and he **claims** that he **worked** in **drugs** and **oil** because they're **respectable** lines of **business**.

2) Nick **contrasts** Daisy's **priorities** with Gatsby's — Gatsby's **"consumed with wonder"** by Daisy and doesn't even notice his **possessions**. He pays **so little attention** that he **"nearly toppled down a flight of stairs"**.

3) **Klipspringer** plays **'Ain't we got fun'** which highlights the **meaninglessness** of all of Gatsby's **possessions** now that he **'has'** Daisy, the only thing of **true value** to him.

> 'Ain't we got fun'
>
> The popular song **jokes** about the **resilience** of the **working class** using the argument that if you already **have nothing**, **no one** can **take** anything **from you**. This song is an **ironic commentary** on Gatsby's meeting with Daisy, and highlights the **excess** and **unhappiness** of the **wealthy Gatsby**, who has **everything except** what he **wants**.

Practice Questions

Q1 There are numerous references to songs and song lyrics throughout *The Great Gatsby*. Using Chapter Five as a starting point, analyse the significance of these references.

Q2 Contrast the portrayal of Gatsby in this chapter and in the rest of the novel. How far do you think that the Gatsby we see in Chapter 5 is the real Gatsby?

"Daisy tumbled short of his dreams... because of the colossal vitality of his illusion"

"Great Scott! It's 1885" "No Doc, it's Great Gatsby, published in 1925..." "Great Scott!" "No. Great. Gatsby." "Great Scott Fitzgerald?" "No! Listen! Gr—eat Gats—by..." "Great Gatsby Scott?" "Oh never mind" "Who's Tom?" "I never said anything about a Tom." "Oh."

Chapter Six

Gatsby and Daisy's affair continues right under Tom's nose, whilst the rumours about Gatsby's past refuse to go away...

Gatsby's Past *is* Revealed...

- **Nick explains** that **Gatsby** is actually **James Gatz** from **North Dakota** who left **home** at a **young age** to **seek his fortune**. Gatsby **changed his name** at **seventeen** when he met **Dan Cody**, a **self-made millionaire**.

- **Tom** is **invited** to one of Gatsby's **parties** and arrives with **Daisy**. Daisy is **offended** by **West Egg** and the **debauchery** of the **party**, while Tom gets the **names** and **addresses** of **pretty women**.

- Gatsby wants **Daisy** to say that she **never loved Tom** so they can "**wipe out**" her **marriage** and **start again**.

1) This chapter raises the **issue** of **why** Gatsby **really wants** Daisy — his **poor upbringing** spurred him on to achieve the **American Dream**, and Daisy **represents** the **class** and **wealth** that he **aspires** to.

2) It's clear that Gatsby's **wealth** does not mean he also has the **manners** and **behaviour** of an **upper-class aristocrat**. The reader **suspects** that Daisy's **unlikely** to want to **leave** the **security** and **respectability** of being married to **Tom**.

Gatsby *was* Created *in the* Pursuit *of the* American Dream

1) The chapter **begins** with an inquisitive reporter turning up on Gatsby's doorstep who hopes that there must be **some truth** in the **rumours** that will make a **good story**.

> *Nick has rearranged the order of events to help the reader understand who Gatsby was and who he might be now.*

- The rumours have made Gatsby "**just short of being news**", and **expanded** Gatsby's **identity** beyond what he could actually be (see p.59).

- Directly after this, Nick reveals **information** found out "**very much later**" about Gatsby's **real history**. This **contrast** encourages the **reader** to draw **comparisons** between the **man** and the **myth**.

- Fitzgerald establishes Gatsby as a **timeless hero** — he's described as a "**son of God**" and some critics have seen him as a **Christ-like figure** (see p.43).

2) **Dan Cody**, a **self-made millionaire**, was young Gatsby's **example** of the American Dream. However, Cody had **questionable morals** — he "**brought back... the savage violence of the frontier brothel and saloon**". Gatsby **followed** Cody's example, achieving his wealth through **immoral means**.

3) Gatsby's **pursuit** of the **American Dream** became a pursuit of **wealth** — his dreams of being a **great man** were **corrupted**.

4) When Gatsby **met Daisy** his dream of **wealth** and **status** was **replaced** by a **dream** of **being with her**. For the older Gatsby she **represents** the **American Dream** and **everything** that he **hopes** to **achieve**.

> *For more on Daisy's role as a symbol of the American Dream see p.13.*

5) It's significant that **Cody's death** was apparently caused by the **treachery** of the **woman** he **loved** — this **foreshadows** Daisy's treachery and **Gatsby's death**.

Class Prejudices *become* Clearer

1) Gatsby's **interactions** with **Tom**, **Mr Sloane** and an **unnamed lady** indicate that **despite** his **wealth** he's **not welcome** in their **society**. Gatsby doesn't **realise** that he wasn't **expected** to **accept** their **invitation** to **dinner**.

2) Gatsby's **behaviour** is **contrasted** with that of the **East Eggers**. Gatsby is **courteous**, **welcoming** the riders and **offering refreshments**. The **East Egg** community accept his **generosity** "**without gratitude**" and leave **without him**. Nick **realises** that Gatsby thinks that "**they cared!**". The **exclamation mark** indicates Nick's **contempt** for the **selfishness** of the **upper classes**.

3) Tom is **contemptuous** towards Gatsby and his failure to **realise** that the lady "**doesn't want him**". He's **appalled** that **Daisy knows** someone like him: "**women run around too much [...] they meet all kinds of crazy fish**".

4) Gatsby's **naivety** of **class prejudice** is also seen in his **vain belief** that Daisy will **abandon** her **status** and **position** to be **with him**. For all his **wealth**, he will **remain working class** and will never be **good enough** for Daisy.

Chapter Six

Daisy attends one of Gatsby's Parties

1) **Daisy** is **escorted** to Gatsby's party by **Tom**, who is **"perturbed"** at her **"running around alone"**. Nick feels that Tom's **"presence"** fills the party with a **"quality of oppressiveness"**, **"unpleasantness"** and **"harshness"** — this party feels much **darker** and more **sinister** than the earlier ones.

2) Daisy is **"appalled"** by the **vulgar behaviour** and **drunken guests** but seems **sadly resigned** to **Tom's involvement** with them. **Tom** is seen to be collecting the **details** of at least one **woman** at the **party**, and Daisy even **offers** her **"gold pencil"** to **him** to make it clear that **she knows** what he's doing.

3) Nick may be **reassessing** the **mood** and **nature** of Gatsby's party through **Daisy's eyes**. He says that it is **"invariably saddening to look through new eyes at things upon which you have expended your own powers of adjustment"** — Daisy's presence reminds **Nick** that he has let himself get **used to** the West Eggers' **hedonistic lifestyle**.

> Nick's **new viewpoint** affects his **narration**. His language is **sparse** and **dark compared** to the **poetic descriptions** that made earlier parties seem **magical** (see p.10 and p.50-51). The **"many-coloured, many-keyed commotion"** makes the **party** sound **confusing** and **discordant**.

Gatsby wants to Recover the Past with Daisy

1) Fitzgerald **presents** Daisy and Tom's **affairs** in **different** ways:

© PARAMOUNT / THE KOBAL COLLECTION

- Daisy **jokes** that she is giving out **"green cards"** to advertise her **availability**. This is a **parody** of Tom's **shameless** and **public flirting**.
- Daisy admires the **movie star**, and Nick notices that the star's **director**, over the course of the evening, slowly leans in for a **"kiss at her cheek"**. This **slow build up matches** Daisy's **affair** with **Gatsby**, which is portrayed in a **chaste** and **romantic** light.

2) Fitzgerald doesn't provide a **first-person account** of **Gatsby** and **Daisy's** current **affair**. Instead, he affords it a **degree** of **privacy** that suggests it is **more respectable** and **sincere** than Tom's **short-lived** and **public 'flings'**:

> The **account** of Gatsby's **first kiss** with Daisy is written in **poetic prose**: **"incomparable milk of wonder"**, **"tuning-fork that had been struck upon a star"**. The **overblown language** shows **Gatsby** at his **most vulnerable** and **pathetic**. Nick is aware of the **"appalling sentimentality"** of Gatsby's language — Gatsby's so **lost** in his **romantic dream** that he **no longer** sees Daisy as a **real person**. But Nick also sees something **deeper**, a **"fragment of lost words"**.

3) Gatsby's **kiss** with Daisy is **narrated** through Nick's **second-person perspective** using the **past perfect** tense — Nick's **narrative voice** emphasises the fact that Gatsby's **first kiss** is something belonging to the **nostalgic past**.

4) The **first time** Gatsby **kissed** Daisy, his **obsession** with her **replaced** all his **other dreams**. Once Gatsby has her, his dream is **over** and he has **no further** ambitions: **"his mind would never romp again like the mind of God"**.

5) Gatsby wants everything to be **"just the way it was before"**, and **won't accept** Nick's assertion that **"You can't repeat the past"**. Gatsby is so **obsessed** with the **past** that he **seems to pay little attention** to the **present**.

Practice Questions

Q1 Reread Nick's account of Gatsby's past. Do you think that Gatsby achieved the American Dream? Give examples from the text in your answer.

Q2 How does the portrayal of Gatsby's love for Daisy persuade the reader to be sympathetic to their affair?

"He wanted to recover something... that had gone into loving Daisy"

Considering James Gatz came up with the character of Gatsby at the age of seventeen, he's a pretty sophisticated fellow — you'd think he'd be more of a cross between Hugh Heffner and Lionel Messi. [Insert joke about ball control here.]

Chapter Seven

The longest of the novel's chapters and things have started hotting up — literally. It's the hottest day of the year...

Tom **Finds Out** about **Daisy's Affair**...

- **Gatsby** stops **holding parties** and **replaces** all of his **servants** to **prevent** any **gossip** about **Daisy's visits**.
- Nick, Gatsby and Jordan go for **lunch** at Tom and Daisy's. Tom **realises** that Daisy and Gatsby are **in love**. They all go to **New York**. Tom stops for **petrol** and **Wilson** reveals that he knows **Myrtle** is **having an affair**.
- In **New York**, Tom **confronts** Gatsby about his **past** and **accuses** him of being a **bootlegger**. Gatsby tells Tom that Daisy **never loved him**, but she claims she **did** and decides to **stay** with **Tom**.
- Daisy and Gatsby **drive** home **ahead** of the others. On the way back they **hit** and **kill Myrtle**. Tom **finds out** that **Gatsby's car** was **involved** in the **accident**. Gatsby tells Nick that **Daisy was driving** but that he'll take the **blame**.

1) Chapter 7 is the **climax** of the **novel** — the **different strands** of the **story** finally **converge** in **Myrtle's dramatic death**.

2) The **conflict** between Tom and Gatsby **finally** comes to the **surface** — their **argument** **reveals flaws** in both of them — Tom's **prejudice** and **bullying** is highlighted, as well as Gatsby's **immoral**, **criminal activities**, and his **inability** to **let go** of the **past**.

3) The **climax** occurs on the **hottest day** of **summer** — the **oppressive heat reflects** the **passion** and **tension** of the characters' **affairs**. The **heat** makes everyone **irritable**, and at a symbolic level it **brings** everything to the **boil**.

Gatsby puts an End to his Parties

1) The **chapter opens** with the news that Gatsby has **stopped** his **parties** and **replaced** his **staff**. The **tone** is **unsettling** and **sinister** — the new butler has a **"villainous face"** and it's **rumoured** that **"the new people weren't servants at all"**. Now **Gatsby** has **achieved** his dream of being with Daisy, the parties **no longer matter** and his **lifestyle** has **"fallen in like a card house at the disapproval in her eyes"**.

2) The **rumours** surrounding Gatsby once made him **mythical** (see p.16 and p.59). However, now he **shies away** from them by **stopping** his **parties** and **replacing** all of his **servants**.

3) The rumours that were once a **"source of satisfaction"**, presumably because he hoped that **Daisy** might **hear** about him, now **threaten** the very **relationship** he has **established** with **Daisy**. If **Long Island society** were to hear about **Daisy's** afternoon visits at **Gatsby's**, his **affair** would be **cut short**.

4) Nick declares that Gatsby's **"career as Trimalchio was over"** when Gatsby **ends** his **parties**. Fitzgerald gives Gatsby a new literary identity as the **modern Trimalchio** of the **American Dream**:

> **Trimalchio**
>
> In Petronius' *Satyricon*, **Trimalchio** is a **former slave** who has made a **fortune** through **hard work** and gained a degree of power. He's **famous** for **holding lavish parties**, but the **glamour** of his **exotic feasts** is **undermined** by the fact that he's **vulgar** and his **display of wealth** is **garish**.

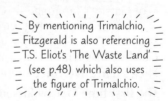

By mentioning Trimalchio, Fitzgerald is also referencing T.S. Eliot's 'The Waste Land' (see p.48) which also uses the figure of Trimalchio.

Trimalchio's story ends with his guests **acting out** his **funeral** for his own entertainment, so Nick's mention of Trimalchio could be seen as **foreshadowing** Gatsby's **death**.

Daisy seems to Want to Stir things Up

In **contrast** to Gatsby's **careful**, **secretive** behaviour, Daisy **appears reckless**:

1) At lunch Daisy **flirts** with Gatsby **openly**, **kissing** him **in front** of Jordan and Nick. Daisy **acts** as if she's in **control**, **ordering** Tom to **"make us a cold drink"**. She **inadvertently reveals** to Tom that she **loves** Gatsby: **"You always look so cool"**. Daisy seems to want to **force** a **confrontation** between Tom and Gatsby.

2) Her **behaviour startles Tom**, who insists they go to **New York**. Tom **demands** to know whether **Nick** and **Jordan** had seen **"that"** (the **flirting**). Tom **avoids** saying what he had **seen** but it's clear that he knows Daisy has been **unfaithful**. He claims he has a **"second sight"** that tells him **"what to do"** — his **reaction** is **impulsive** and **instinct-driven**.

Chapter Seven

Tom and Wilson Realise they've Lost Control of their Wives

1) On the way to **New York**, Tom is **forced** to stop for **petrol** at Wilson's **garage**. Fitzgerald uses this **meeting** to **juxtapose** the **two men** whose **wives** are **having affairs**.

> - **Tom realises** he is **losing control** of 'his' **women** — he **suspects Daisy** is having an **affair** and finds out that Wilson might force **Myrtle** to move "**West**". The **realisation** that the **women** in his life had "**some sort of life apart from him**" makes Tom feel "**hot whips of panic**".
> - Wilson's **discovery** of his **wife's affair** has made him **physically sick**.

© PARAMOUNT / THE KOBAL COLLECTION

2) Wilson **internalises** his **grief**, while Tom **expresses it** — he steps "**on the accelerator**". Tom's speed **symbolises** his anger but it also **speeds up** the **plot** towards its **climax**.

3) Myrtle is **absent** from this **meeting**, which **symbolises** that she has no control over her **destiny**. She looks out through "**one of the windows over the garage**" because she's "**locked in up there**". Wilson makes **decisions for her**: "**she's going whether she wants to or not**". Wilson and Tom both seem to **treat** their **wives** as **possessions**.

Tom Confronts Gatsby about his Affair

1) At the Plaza hotel Tom forces an **argument** by **addressing Gatsby** in an **increasingly hostile** manner.

> Tom addresses Gatsby formally as "**Mr Gatsby**", making it **clear** he **doesn't want** to be **friendly**. Tom **aggressively** calls Gatsby "**Mr Nobody from Nowhere**" to **emphasise** how **unimportant** he thinks Gatsby is.

2) Tom can't **bear** that Daisy is **attracted** to Gatsby, with his '**new money**' and **lack** of **upper-class breeding** — Tom sees this **threat** to his **marriage** as a **threat** to his idea of **civilisation** — for Tom, "**sneering at family life**" is the first step towards "**intermarriage between black and white**", which for him **symbolises** the **breakdown** of **order**.

3) Both men try to **claim** Daisy as their **own**, without **respecting** her **feelings**. Tom says that she "**gets foolish ideas in her head and doesn't know what she's doing**" and Gatsby **dismisses** her **opinion** because she's "**all excited now**".

4) Fitzgerald **stresses** the **importance** of **time** in the **confrontation**. Gatsby wants to **rewrite** the **past** and insists that Daisy tells Tom that she "**never loved**" him. However, Tom **invokes** his **history** with Daisy to **re-ignite** her **feelings** for him.

5) Daisy is **shaken** by the **truth** about Gatsby's **past**, which highlights her **snobbery** and **materialism**. She **rejects Gatsby** because he's not of her **class** — he's a **criminal** whose **whole life** has been an **act**.

Gatsby's Car Kills Myrtle in an Accident

1) Nick's **narration** of the **return journey** to **East Egg** is **interrupted** by **details** from **Michaelis'** inquest report. This **change** in **perspective** gives some **narrative distance** to the **horror** of **Myrtle's death**.

2) Myrtle's **death** is described in **shocking language**: "**her left breast was swinging loose like a flap**". Myrtle's body is **sexualised** even in **death**, highlighting the **tragic loss** of her "**tremendous vitality**".

3) The **narrative** shifts back to **first-person perspective** for the final sections of the chapter to describe the **reactions** to **Myrtle's death**. Wilson and Tom react with **horror**, but Daisy, who **committed** the **crime**, shows **no emotion**. Gatsby is **emotionally detached**, **waiting** for a **sign** from **Daisy**. Daisy's **protective retreat** into her big house **returns Gatsby** to his **isolated** "**vigil**", echoing his first appearance in **Chapter 1**.

Practice Questions

Q1 'Tom's hatred of Gatsby is caused more by the fact that he's "Mr Nobody from Nowhere", rather than the fact that he's been having an affair with Daisy.' To what extent do you agree with this statement?

Q2 Do you think Daisy would have been happy to leave Tom for Gatsby if she hadn't found out about his criminal activities? Do you think they would have had a happy relationship together?

"So we drove on toward death through the cooling twilight."

"What?" "So we drove on toward death" "WHAT?" "SO WE DROVE ON TOWARD DEATH!" "Oh sorry, I thought you said 'deaf'" hahaHaHaHAHA... Straight from my dad's joke collection that was. Guaranteed at least fifty years old or your money back...

Chapter Eight

The story builds towards its tragic conclusion as Wilson assumes that Gatsby killed his wife.

Gatsby's **Dream** is **Dead**...

- **Gatsby waits all night** outside the **Buchanans' house** in case **Daisy needs him**, but **nothing happens**.
- Gatsby **tells Nick** the **truth** about his **past** and his **relationship** with **Daisy**.
- Nick goes to **work** where he receives a **phone call** from **Jordan**. He **makes excuses** not to **see** her.
- Nick **describes events** that occurred just **after Myrtle's death**, and hints that Wilson **headed to Gatsby's house**.
- Nick **returns** from work and finds that Gatsby has been **killed**. Wilson's **body** is found **nearby**.

The chapter **begins** at the **end** of **summer**, which **coincides** with the **ending** of Gatsby's **dream**, his **love affair** with Daisy and his **life**. Fitzgerald uses various **narrative techniques** in this chapter to **build suspense**:

1) The chapter is **divided** into **short segments** to suggest that the **novel** is **building up** to a **climax**.

2) Nick uses a **series** of **incomplete accounts** to **increase** the **tension** — because the story is **told** from the **point of view** of a **range** of **characters**, the reader **doesn't know** what to **believe**. **Withholding information** increases the **mystery**.

3) Fitzgerald creates a **cliffhanger** at the end of the **chapter** — Gatsby's **dead** but it's not **clear** how.

Gatsby *tells Nick his* Real History

1) Chapter 8 opens **ominously** — Nick **can't sleep** and shifts between **nightmares** and **"grotesque"** reality:

> Around dawn Nick **walks over** to **Gatsby's house** to find **Gatsby** has **neglected** his **home** while he has been **seeing Daisy**. The **darkness contrasts** with the **bright lights** of former times and the **"splash upon the keys of a ghostly piano"** in the **dark** is like an **echo** of **past parties**.

2) Now that Gatsby's house is **empty** and **dark**, and the fictional persona of 'Jay Gatsby' has **"broken up like glass against Tom's hard malice"** Nick declares that the **"long secret extravaganza"** of the **rumours** and **parties** is over. The **illusion** of the **Great Gatsby** is **shattered** — Gatsby's **no longer** 'great', but is **revealed** to be **just a man**.

3) Gatsby **can't accept** that his **dream** is **dead**. He **talks** to Nick about **Daisy** as a **way** of **keeping** his **dream alive**. Nick's references to Daisy's **wealth** and **status** — **"the bought luxury of star-shine"**, **"a person from much the same strata as herself"** — implies that Gatsby is **attracted** to what Daisy **stands for**, rather than **who she is**.

4) Gatsby wasted his **great ability** to achieve his **dreams** when he **discarded** his other **ambitions** to chase the **dream** of Daisy. He thinks there's no use **"doing great things if I could have a better time telling her what I was going to do"**.

5) It's **suggested** that Gatsby **only wanted** Daisy because, like the **"grail"**, she was unobtainable. Gatsby's **tendency to dream** means he **always wants more**. The reference to the **grail** links Gatsby to **medieval knights** who followed the **strict code** of **chivalry** in completing **dangerous quests** and **selflessly worshipping** their 'lady' at a **distance**.

6) Gatsby **repeatedly suggests** he's **unworthy** of **Daisy**. Nick's claim that Gatsby is **"worth the whole damn bunch"** contradicts his 'unworthiness' and highlights the **problems** of a **class-based society**.

Nick Grows Tired *of the Egg Community*

1) Nick now sees through the **veneer** of 'polite society' and is **repulsed** by their **lack** of **care** and **shallow behaviour**.

2) Nick's description of the **society** Daisy grew up in is **critical** of her **"artificial world"** full of **"cheerful snobbery"**:

> Nick suggests she was part of the **leisure class** that **"drifted here and there"** listening to the **"hopeless comment of the 'Beale Street Blues'"**, a song about the impact of **prohibition** on **African-American culture**. The **social commentary** of the **music** goes **unheard** by the **upper classes** and the **image** of a **"hundred pairs of golden and silver slippers"** highlights the **huge social inequality** between **different races** and **classes**.

3) **Jordan** is also a **part** of that **society** and **Nick's decision** to **break off** their **relationship** reflects his **growing distaste** for the **upper classes**. Nick's **treatment** of **Jordan** is **cruel**, especially because Jordan's **cool exterior** has **fallen away** leaving her **vulnerable** — her voice is **"harsh and dry"**. Nick gives Jordan vague excuses why he can't see her — this lack of **openness** is **characteristic** of his **inability** to form **emotional connections** with **other people** (see p.27).

4) Nick takes a **moralistic** stance towards Gatsby's **criminal activities** and **lies**, claiming to have **"disapproved of him from beginning to end"**. However, Nick still recognises that Gatsby's **greatness** comes from **following** his **dream**.

Chapter Eight

Fitzgerald *draws* Parallels *between* Gatsby *and* Wilson

1) Nick **interrupts** his **narrative** to relate **Michaelis's description** of what happened at the garage **after Myrtle's death**. This helps juxtapose **Gatsby's** and **Wilson's characters**.

2) Both men have had **sleepless nights**, with Gatsby keeping a **"vigil"** at **Daisy's window** and **Wilson** looking out of his **window** at the **eyes** of **T.J. Eckleburg**, which he sees as the **image** of **God's judgement**:

   - George thinks that **T.J. Eckleburg represents God**, but **Michaelis** tries to persuade him that the **eyes** have **no spiritual meaning** — **"'That's an advertisement,' Michaelis assured him."**
   - In some ways, Gatsby makes the **same mistake** in **seeing** his life's 'meaning' in **Daisy** — he's **fantasised** about her for **so long** he's **lost sight** of who she actually is. Nick's comment — **"what a grotesque thing a rose is"** — reminds the reader that an **object** only has the **beauty** and **value** that the **viewer gives** to it.

3) Both **Gatsby** and **Wilson** are **dreamers** who **idealise** the women they love, so it's **significant** that their **final nights** are **sleepless** — their **dreams** are **over**.

4) In the **shallow**, **materialistic world** that Fitzgerald portrays, **dreamers** inevitably **lose out** to **privileged** men like **Tom**.

Gatsby's Dream *finally* Dies

1) Fitzgerald **describes** the dawn **light "grey-turning, gold-turning"** to suggest that the events of the novel are '**on the turn**'.

   The **bright colours** of summer are **replaced** with **"grey"** light and **"blue leaves"**. The **hint** of **"gold"** in the **"gold-turning"** light could **represent** Gatsby's continued **delusion** that Daisy is still **waiting** for **him** and that things will **turn around again**.

© PARAMOUNT / THE KOBAL COLLECTION

2) Gatsby is **faithful** to **Daisy** until the **end**. He **dies** because he takes the **blame** for her **carelessness** — Wilson **kills him** because he believes **Gatsby** is **responsible** for Myrtle's **death**, when in fact Daisy is **responsible**. The fact that he **dies** in her place **emphasises** his **nobility**.

3) However, **Daisy** doesn't show the **same commitment** to Gatsby:

   Gatsby's **last sight** of Daisy is of her standing for a **minute** at her **window** before she **"turned out the light"**. Gatsby describes the scene **"wanly" without** Nick's **poetic flourishes**. It's a **simple** but **intense image** of Gatsby's **return to isolation** — Daisy's act of **turning off** the **light** symbolises the fact that she has thrown his **dreams** into **darkness**, because Gatsby **dreams** of Daisy are so **closely tied** to **light** (specifically the **green light**).

4) Gatsby is **killed** on the first day of **autumn** which **symbolises** the fact that he **refuses** to **accept** the **passage of time** and **keeps trying** to **recapture** the **past**. He **insists** on using the **pool** even though the season is **inappropriate**. He **clings** to **summer** and **can't accept** that it's **over** in the same way he **clings** to his **dream** and **can't accept** that **Daisy** has **left him**.

Practice Questions

Q1 Do you think that Nick makes a fair assessment in saying that "'Jay Gatsby' had broken up like glass against Tom's hard malice"? Back up your answer with examples from the text.

Q2 Using Chapter 8 as a starting point, analyse the role of weather and the seasons in dictating the mood of the novel. Back up your answer with examples from the text.

Q3 'Daisy never loved Tom or Gatsby — she was only ever in love with money and the comfort that came with it.' To what extent do you agree with this statement? Refer to the text in your answer.

"They're a rotten crowd... You're worth the whole damn bunch put together"

That's what I shout when I'm trying to reassure my Golden Delicious. He's very insecure and thinks I've got a thing for rotten grapes... I don't think he really understands how wine is made. I love grapes, but don't tell him — he'll be utterly devastated.

Chapter Nine

Fitzgerald spends the final chapter tying up loose ends and summarising the novel's key message...

Nick **Picks Up** the **Pieces** After Gatsby's Death...

- Nick describes the events after **Gatsby's death**. He **organises** a **funeral** but only Gatsby's **father**, Owl Eyes, a few servants and the postman attend.
- Nick meets **Jordan** and they **talk about** why their **relationship ended**.
- **Tom reveals** that he **told Wilson** that **Gatsby** was **driving** the car that **killed** Myrtle.
- On Nick's **last night** before he **moves back** to the **Midwest** he reflects that Gatsby believed he was **running towards** his **dream**, and didn't realise it was already **behind him**.

Despite the **recent dramatic events nobody** has **changed**:

1) **Tom** and **Daisy leave town** and **carry on** with their lives **as if nothing** has **happened**.
2) **Nick** still seems to **think** that he's **morally superior** to most of **East coast society**.
3) **Jordan** has tried to **resume** her **cold exterior** and Nick suspects she's **lying** when she tells him she's **engaged**.

Gatsby's Funeral reveals the **Emptiness** of the **American Dream**

1) The characters' **reactions** to **Gatsby's death** give a **final insight** into their **personality** and **relationship** with him:

- **Nick** tries hard to **"get somebody"** for **Gatsby's funeral** and sees himself as the **only person** **"on Gatsby's side"**. Nick **empathises** with Gatsby and **distances himself** from **East coast society**.
- **Daisy** doesn't even send a **"message or a flower"**. Her **silence** and **absence** suggest she wants to **forget** her **involvement** with Gatsby and **move on** with her **life**. This **emphasises** that she's **shallow**, **weak** and **careless**.
- **Wolfshiem** refuses to **"get mixed up in"** Gatsby's **death** and **funeral** in case a **criminal connection** is **drawn** between them. Wolfshiem claims that it's **better** to show someone **friendship** while they're **alive**.
- **Klipspringer**, **"the boarder"**, **represents** the **guests** who enjoyed Gatsby's **hospitality** but **didn't care** about him. Klipspringer is so **uncaring** that he **misses** the **funeral** for a **"picnic or something"**.
- Gatsby's **father**, Henry C. Gatz, asks Nick to **delay the funeral** so that he **can travel from the Midwest** to attend. However, **even** he is taken in by the **grand display** of Gatsby's **material success** and is **proud** of his **son's achievements** — he **doesn't realise** his son **never achieved** his **dream**.

2) **Gatsby built himself up** from **nothing** to a position of **relative wealth** and **power** and therefore could be seen to **epitomise** the **American Dream**. However, the **poor attendance** of his **funeral** shows that he had **very few close friends**, which **highlights** the **hollowness** and **emotional cost** of his version of the **American Dream**.

Nick **Returns** to the **Theme of Geography**

1) In the **final chapter** Nick **concludes** that **"this has been a story of the West"** because all of the **main characters** are from the **West** and **"possessed some deficiency... which made us subtly unadaptable to Eastern life."**

2) Nick's view of **East** and **West** changes through the **novel** (see p.57) so that by the end he has **exchanged** his view of the **West** as the **"ragged edge of the universe"** (Chapter 1) that was full of **"bored, sprawling, swollen towns"** (Chapter 9) to a childlike nostalgia for **"my Middle West"** that takes him back to **"my youth"**. He recognises that **"I am part of that"** and **comes to terms** with his **identity** as a **Westerner** in a way the other characters **couldn't**.

3) In **contrast**, Nick says that **after Gatsby's death** the **East coast** has become **"haunted"** and **"distorted"** for him:

Nick **describes** the **East** in a **flat**, **morbid** vocabulary to emphasise his distaste — the **wind** carries the **scent** of **"brittle leaves"** in **bonfires** and **blows** through laundry that is **"stiff"**. The words **"brittle"** and **"stiff"** reflect the **difficulty** Nick seems to have had in making **strong relationships** in a **cold** and **unfriendly society**.

4) Nick **characterises** the **East** as a **place** that **lacks morals**. It plays host to a series of **"gleaming, dazzling parties"** that create the impression of a **glittering surface** with very little **depth**. This can be **contrasted** with the **deliberate** way Nick describes the **twinkle** of the **"real snow, our snow"** that he recalls from his **childhood** in the **West**.

Chapter Nine

Nick's Moral Superiority is Challenged

1) The novel's **ending inverts** the very **beginning** of the book — Nick's **initial claims** that he **doesn't judge anyone** and that he's **moral and honest** are **proven** to be **false**, even if Nick himself **doesn't realise** it.

© Everett Collection / Rex Features

2) Nick is probably at his **most judgmental** in this chapter, **specifically** declaring that Tom and Daisy "**were careless people**" because of they way "**they smashed up things and creatures and then retreated back into their money**".

3) However, his **emotionally charged meeting** with Jordan results in the realisation that Nick himself is a "**careless**" person. Jordan says that she was "**wrong**" to think that Nick was an "**honest, straightforward person**":

> Jordan picks up the **analogy** about "**careless drivers**" again (p.54), saying that a "**bad driver was only safe until she met another bad driver**". **Jordan** calls Nick a "**bad driver**" — she's comparing their **relationship** to a **car crash**.

The Last Lines Sum Up the Message of the Novel

1) Nick **closes** the **novel** with characteristic **poetic prose**:

> Nick sees the **green light** as the "**unattainable dream**". He thinks that Gatsby would **never** have **achieved his dream** of the **future** because it was rooted in the **past**.

> Gatsby believed in the green light, the orgastic future that year by year recedes before us. It eluded us then, but that's no matter — tomorrow we will run faster, stretch out our arms further ...
> And one fine morning —
> So we beat on, boats against the current, borne back ceaselessly into the past.

> Nick knows the **green light** can **never** be **reached**, so his **message** never **reaches** its **conclusion, interrupted** by **long dashes** (—) and **ellipses** (...).

> Gatsby tried to **relive** the **past** with Daisy but **escape** his **past** life in the West. This is an **impossible dilemma**. Nick suggests that this is a **universal problem** — "**we**" all try to **fight against** the "**current**" of time.

> Nick uses an **unusual word** (see p.50) that makes the future seem **unfamiliar** and **exciting**.

2) Nick links Gatsby's fate to that of America by **comparing** Gatsby's dreams to the experiences of the first **European settlers** in **America**. Nick thinks that Gatsby **shared** the **same sense** of **hope**, **wonder** and **possibility** in pursuing his dreams that the **settlers** felt when they **experienced** the "**fresh, green breast of the new world**" for the first time.

3) When America was **founded** it tried to **distance itself** from the **traditional class system** it **left behind** in Europe, by **promising people** that **anything** was **possible**, **regardless** of their **background**. The **emphasis** on '**old money**' versus '**new money**' shows that the **social hierarchy** still exists in **America** — the **dream** has **failed**. Likewise, Gatsby **fails** to **overcome** the **class barrier** which **separates** him and Daisy, which **shows** that he can't **escape** his **past**.

4) Nick recognises that **Gatsby** represents **humanity's endless capacity** for **hope**, even when **all the evidence** suggests **no one** can **escape** the **past**. The **image** of **boats** in the "**ceaseless**" **tide** captures the **mixture** of **futility** and **hope**.

Practice Questions

Q1 "Then wear the gold hat, if that will move her; / If you can bounce high, bounce for her too, / Till she cry 'Lover, gold-hatted, high-bouncing lover, / I must have you!'"
Explore the ways in which the epigraph to *The Great Gatsby* relates to the themes of the novel.

Q2 In what ways is the story of Gatsby's life also the story of America since the arrival of the first explorers?

"So we beat on, boats against the current, borne back ceaselessly into the past"

Not the most cheery of endings but it's better than 'They all lived happily ever after.' It's also one of the most famous last lines in American literature, although I prefer the ending of the OED: zyxt — (obsolete) second-person singular past tense of to zi ("see"). Classic...

Jay Gatsby

Welcome ladies and gentlemen to the show you've all been waiting for... Yes, I give you — The Great Gatsby. Gatsby's life isn't exactly a lie, but it is an illusion. He spends the entire book pretending to be someone he's not.

Gatsby is a Man of Mystery

1) Although the **novel** is **titled after Gatsby**, Fitzgerald doesn't **introduce** him in person until **Chapter 3**, and we don't learn his real story until much later. This increases the **intrigue** and **mystery** about him.

2) Nick says in **Chapter 1** that only Gatsby was **"exempt"** from his **"unaffected scorn"**. This encourages the reader to **find out** why Nick thinks Gatsby is so **special**.

3) **Rumours** surround Gatsby's **past** and **present**. For the **first half** of the novel the **only information** provided about Gatsby is **outlandish stories**, such as that he's a **"cousin of Kaiser Wilhelm's"**, **"a German spy"** and **"an Oxford man"**.

4) The fact that Gatsby's **real back story** isn't as **mysterious** or **glamorous** as he **makes out, heightens the tragedy** of his **death** — he became **successful** through a combination of **luck** and **hard work**.

© PARAMOUNT / THE KOBAL COLLECTION

Gatsby Created his own Identity

> Gatsby's 'schedule' is a parody of Benjamin Franklin's 'scheme of employment'. Franklin was a self-made man of working-class origins.

1) **Jay Gatsby** is actually a **creation** of **James Gatz**, a **seventeen**-year-old **farm boy** from **North Dakota**.

2) James Gatz **"invented just the sort of Jay Gatsby that a seventeen-year-old boy would be likely to invent"**. His **persona** is **everything** a seventeen-year-old boy **dreams of being**, but it is just an **illusion**.

3) Gatsby's **success** is the result of his **ability** to **reinvent himself** and be **perceived** as he **wants**. He **designs** his **entire life** to **attract Daisy**, but when Gatsby sees her **disgust** at his parties, he reinvents himself **again**.

4) Because he successfully rewrote his **past**, Gatsby believes that he can rewrite his **relationship with Daisy** as well. He wants it to be **the same** as it was **before** she **married Tom** — Gatsby's a **Romantic idealist** (see p.48) rather than a **realist**. He stays **faithful** to the **dream** of Daisy, never realising that he's in love with a dream.

5) Gatsby's **single-minded pursuit** of his dream helps the reader to **sympathise** with him, despite the fact that he's **mysterious** and **elusive**. His **hope** and **creativity** are **inspiring**. However, they also lead to his eventual **downfall**. In this way, Gatsby could be interpreted as a **tragic hero** who is **destroyed** by his fatal **flaw**.

The Man and the Act are very Different

Because Gatsby **rarely** lets his **mask fall**, it's **difficult** to **work out** where the **man ends** and the **act begins**:

> The novel's title sounds like a magician's act, emphasising the fact that Gatsby has created an illusion.

THE ACT	THE MAN
• He **lived** the **life** of a **"young rajah"**.	• He **worked** as a **fisherman** before **joining Cody** on his **yacht**.
• **"Every Allied government"** gave him a **decoration** in the **war**.	• He has an **"authentic"** looking **medal** from **Montenegro** and he **"did extraordinarily well in the war"**.
• He was an **"Oxford man"**.	• He **only attended Oxford** for **"five months"**.
• He **inherited money** from his **family**.	• **Dan Cody** left him **money** but he **never received** it.
• He **"was in the drug business"**.	• He owned **drug stores** but **"sold grain alcohol over the counter"**.

Throughout the novel there are **hints** that Gatsby **isn't** who he **claims** to be, for example:

• He tries to **conceal** his **working-class** background by adopting **phrases** like **"old sport"**, but this sounds **forced** and **unnatural**. His **limited vocabulary** makes him sound **inarticulate** — e.g. **"interesting people [...] People who do interesting things. Celebrated people"**. Nick comments on his use of **"threadbare"** and **overused phrases**.

• He **doesn't realise** that Mr Sloane doesn't want him to come for supper — he **fails** to understand **etiquette** .

Jay Gatsby

Gatsby is *Isolated* from *Other People*

1) Because Gatsby is so **concerned** with **maintaining** his **created persona**, he keeps his **distance** with **most characters** and doesn't let his **guard down**. Nick describes him as being in **"complete isolation"**.

2) This explains his **aloofness** at parties — until Daisy attends, he **doesn't drink**, **dance** or **pair off**. Nick reinforces this when he says **"No one swooned backward on Gatsby, and no French bob touched Gatsby's shoulder"**.

3) At parties, Gatsby stands **"alone on the marble steps"**. This makes him seem **God-like**, **watching** the crowds from **above**. When **Daisy** finally comes to a party he **mingles** with the **crowd** and **loses** his **God-like status**.

4) Gatsby **hides** behind a **mask**, which **prevents** him from making **personal connections** with people — he only tells Nick his **real history** when his adopted persona has been **destroyed** and he has **nothing left to lose**: **"'Jay Gatsby' had broken up like glass"**.

5) Only Nick, Owl Eyes, Henry Gatz, a few servants and the postman attend Gatsby's **funeral**, in spite of the fact that guests used to attend his parties **"by the hundreds"**. Daisy doesn't even **bother sending "a message or a flower"**.

He *Represents* the *Corruption* of the *American Dream*

Fitzgerald used **one man's story** to make an **important point** about how the **American Dream** had been **corrupted**:

1) Gatsby **achieves** the **American Dream** of coming from a **poor working-class background** to obtain **great wealth** and **success**, but he has to **completely reinvent himself**.

2) He changes his **name** to **escape his past** — 'Gatz' is a **German** name, but 'Gatsby' sounds more **English**. Gatsby **doesn't** just want to be **rich**, he wants to belong to the **upper classes**, and he feels that he has to **conceal** his real background and **adopt** the **persona** of an **eccentric aristocrat** to be **accepted**.

3) This shows that the American Dream has been **corrupted** and that it's **not** within **everyone's grasp** — you have to **become someone else** in order to **achieve** it.

4) Gatsby's **dream** of **obtaining Daisy fails** because of his class, which suggests that the American Dream is no longer **feasible**.

5) Gatsby's **dream** of an **idealised Daisy falls away** to reveal the **corruption** that **money causes**, which also reinforces the idea that the American Dream has been **replaced** by the **selfish** and **immoral pursuit** of **wealth**.

Fitzgerald used his own *Experience* to *Create* the character of *Gatsby*

Many critics have **suggested** that **Gatsby** was **based** on **one side** of **Fitzgerald's** personality, while **Nick** was based on the **other** (see page 27).

1) Both Fitzgerald and Gatsby **idolised** the **rich** and **strived** to become **one of them**. Gatsby's lifestyle **mirrors** Fitzgerald's **celebrity status** and his **lavish parties**.

2) Like Gatsby, Fitzgerald was **driven** by his **love** for a woman who **symbolised** everything that he **wanted**.

3) The **focus** of Fitzgerald's **affections**, Zelda, placed **great importance** on **wealth**, like Daisy, and **rejected** Fitzgerald until he had **enough money**. Gatsby was forced to **make his fortune** before Daisy **considered reuniting** with him.

Practice Questions

Q1 'Just as Daisy needs to be adored, Gatsby needs to be acknowledged for his wealth, success and greatness.' To what extent do you agree with this statement? Refer to the text in your answer.

Q2 How would you interpret the novel's title? Give reasons for your answer.

"Just the sort of Jay Gatsby that a seventeen-year-old boy would be likely to invent"

So basically I reckon that the moral of the story is don't dream big, be a realist, don't look back into the past and know your place — how pessimistic... I dared to dream and then, one day, I ended up at CGP. And what's more, I've yet to find myself dead on a lilo...

Nick Carraway

Nick thinks pretty highly of himself... it's just a shame that nobody else seems to agree. It's interesting having a narrator who's also a character, because your personal opinions about the character affect how you interpret their narration.

Nick Changes Over the Course of the Novel

At the Beginning Nick is...

1) **Very traditional** — he's from a **well-off family** in the **Midwest** and has lived a life of **"privilege"**. Nick's **upbringing** and **education** (at Yale) has made him quite **conservative**.

2) **Highly moral** — he thinks that he's **"honest"** and says he has **"a sense of the fundamental decencies"**.

3) **Naïve** — he thinks he's **above** the **corruption** and **materialism** around him and can **remain immune** to it.

4) **Open minded** — he **moves** East because his **experiences** in the **War** have **broadened** his **perspectives** and he **couldn't settle** in the West on his return. He's **simultaneously attracted** to and **disgusted** by **Eastern life**, but maintains that he's **tolerant** and reserves **"all judgements"**.

Initially Nick just **observes** the corruption of the East, but he **changes** as he's **sucked** into the **world** he's **observing**.

At the End Nick is...

© ITV/Rex Features

1) **Judgemental** — he becomes **increasingly** judgemental as the plot continues, and finally he **condemns** Tom and Daisy as **"careless people"** who **"smashed up things"**.

2) **Careless** — Jordan **accuses** Nick of being a **"bad driver"** — she thinks he's guilty of **carelessness**, the very thing he **accuses** Tom and Daisy of.

3) **Morally Ambiguous** — he **helps** Gatsby to have an **affair** with Daisy.

4) **Disillusioned** — he wants to **move back** to the traditional **West**. He **realises** that it's **hopeless** to try and **escape** the **past**.

He's the First-Person Narrator of the Novel

Nick has many characteristics that make him an **effective narrator**:

1) Nick **distances himself** from the **action**, so that he can **better comment** on it. He **observes**, but doesn't want to **get involved** or be **observed himself**. He wants **"to look squarely at every one and yet to avoid all eyes"**.

2) He's not quite **outside** or **inside** either Gatsby's or the Buchanans' **social circle**, so he has an **ideal perspective**.

3) He's a **good listener** and **doesn't judge people** (aloud) so they're **inclined** to **tell him things**. However he also **criticises** them **behind** their **backs**, and his **opinions** help **develop** the **characters** in the novel:

> E.g. when Daisy confides in Nick that she's had a **"very bad time"** and has felt **"utterly abandoned"**, he stays **quiet**, only speaking to **encourage** her to say more. In writing, he condemns it as **"basic insincerity"**.

However, even with this **distance** Nick's still just a **character** — he's **biased** and **unreliable**:

1) We only ever get Nick's **subjective perspective**. Nick says that he thinks life is **best** **"looked at from a single window"** which suggests that Nick might not be looking at the **whole picture** — he could be sacrificing **truth** and **accuracy** for simplicity.

See page 47 for more on Nick as a narrator.

2) He's **naïve** and **easily persuaded** by **surface appearances**. For example, he listens to Gatsby's **stories** about his **past** with **"incredulity"**, but when Gatsby **shows** him a medal he immediately **believes "it was all true"**.

3) Nick tends to **exaggerate** and use **sentimental** images, e.g. **"the tuning-fork that had been struck upon a star"**. This could imply that he ignores the **truth** to make the story more **exciting** or **romantic**.

Nick Carraway

There's some evidence to suggest that Nick may be gay or bisexual, e.g. his encounter with Mr McKee in Chapter 2. This could explain his lack of commitment.

Nick's a *Romantic* but he *Can't Commit*

1) Nick places **great value** on **love** — this is why he **helps** Gatsby have an **affair** with Daisy. He sees their affair as **romantic**, not **immoral**. He never blames or **judges** Gatsby's pursuit of Daisy and admires his "**romantic readiness**".

2) He invents **romantic back stories**, e.g. imagining "**sumptuous and romantic apartments**" above Wilson's garage.

3) However, he can't **commit** to any **relationships** of **his own**. Nick only **breaks it off** with a girl **back home** when it's **clear** that **Jordan's interested** in him. One of the reasons Nick **moved** East to was to **avoid** "**being rumoured into marriage**".

4) He's **concerned** about **appearances**. For example, he lets a "**short affair**" with a girl in New York "**blow quietly away**" because her brother doesn't like it. He claims that he **doesn't want anyone** to "**know or disapprove**". This suggests that being **seen** to do the **right thing** is more important to him than **actually doing** the right thing.

5) Nick struggles to **make connections** with people. He **fantasises** about **entering the lives** of **New York women**, but he **never acts** on his **desires**, despite his "**haunting loneliness**".

6) Possibly, Nick realises that if he **does act** on his desires then his **romantic dreams** would **fall short** of the **reality**.

7) The only **real romantic relationship** Nick has in West Egg is with **Jordan** and it's very **complicated**:

- Nick is both **attracted** to and **contemptuous** of Jordan, which reflects how he feels about **Eastern life**. He likes her **sophistication** but not her **carelessness**, and **breaks up** with her when he **grows sick** of the East.
- When Nick ends the relationship, he says that he was still "**Angry, and half in love with her, and tremendously sorry**" — this could also represent **Nick's attitude** towards **society** on the **East Coast**.
- Nick's **behaviour** towards Jordan could be seen as **unnecessarily cruel** — his **actions**, such as "**trying to ingratiate**" himself to her aunt, **imply** that he's **serious** about her, but he **ends their relationship** just as it **starts to get serious**. He **lies** to her, telling her "**I want to see you too**", rather than telling her how he **really feels**.

Nick *Represents One Side* of *Fitzgerald's* personality

The **two main characters** in the novel, Gatsby and Nick, **represent two parts** of **Fitzgerald's personality**, as he **frequently** used his **own experiences** to create more **realistic characters** (see page 1):

1) Whilst Gatsby is a **reflection** of Fitzgerald's **celebrity lifestyle**, Nick **represents** Fitzgerald's **quiet** and **reflective side**.

2) Like Nick, Fitzgerald was a **university-educated**, **traditional Midwesterner** with an **upper-middle-class** background.

3) Both Nick and Fitzgerald were simultaneously **attracted** to and **repulsed** by the **debauchery** of the **East** and each of them **saw through** the **seductive Eastern lifestyle** to the **moral emptiness** beneath.

4) Because of these **similarities**, it's quite **difficult** to **distinguish** where **Fitzgerald the author** and **Nick the narrator** become **separate**. Fitzgerald **wrote** the novel **through Nick's eyes**, so it's **difficult to tell** their **two voices apart**:

- Nick and Fitzgerald have **different motivations** — whilst Nick **tries not to judge** and **implies** that the novel **isn't didactic**, Fitzgerald **wants the reader** to **make judgements** and **draw conclusions** from the text.
- When Nick makes **insightful comments** that could **apply** to the **world outside of the text**, such as his **analysis** of the **green light in Chapter 9**, it's fair to **assume** that Nick is acting as Fitzgerald's **voice**. He **sums up** the novel to help the reader consider its **message**.

'Didactic' refers to something that teaches a moral lesson

Practice Questions

Q1 "I was going to... become again that most limited of all specialists, the 'well-rounded man.'" Assess whether Nick achieves his ambition to become a "well-rounded man" during his time in West Egg.

Q2 Do you think that Nick's traditional values are corrupted during his time in the East?

"I am one of the few honest people that I have ever known"

Oh are you Nick? Are you really? I think that you're a liar and a fraud and a part of the Rebel Alliance and a traitor! Take him away! Oh I'm just being harsh now, he's really just a bit arrogant... I'm not arrogant at all, and that's why I'm better than him. Fact.

Daisy Buchanan

Daisy, Daisy, give me an answer do — I'm half crazy, all for the love of you. It won't be a stylish marriage, I can't afford a carriage, but you'd look sweet on the seat of a bicycle built for two. What's that — you've already married Tom? Rats.

Daisy is *Charming*, but she's also *Shallow* and *Weak*

© PARAMOUNT / THE KOBAL COLLECTION

1) Daisy's the main **female character**. She's **unhappily married** to Tom and has an **affair** with Gatsby.

2) Daisy **represents perfection** to Gatsby because she has the **wealth, class, charm** and **sophistication** that Gatsby has **wanted** all of his life.

3) She's **charming** and **beautiful**. She could be seen as a **romantic idealist** like Gatsby, because she **idealises** the **past**.

4) She's also **selfish, shallow, weak** and **materialistic**. She doesn't seem **worthy** of being the **object** of Gatsby's **affection** and **dreams**.

5) She needs to be adored and her **charming behaviour** is **designed** to get **people's attention** — she cries "**ecstatically**" when she hears that there are people in Chicago who **miss her**. This reinforces the idea that she's **needy** and **attention seeking**.

6) Daisy was supposedly **based on** two **real women** in Fitzgerald's life — an old love called **Ginevra King** and his **wife Zelda**. Both Ginevra and Zelda (initially) **rejected** Fitzgerald because he wasn't **wealthy enough**.

She's a *Seductive* character...

> The name Daisy also links her with the flower — this could imply that she's fresh and innocent, or it could suggest that she's not as special as she appears.

1) Gatsby's completely **obsessed** with Daisy, and at times **Nick** and **Tom** also seem **enchanted**.

2) Much of Daisy's **power** lies in her **voice**. Gatsby says that her **voice** is "**full of money**", and Nick thinks that there's "**an excitement in her voice... a singing compulsion, a whispered 'Listen'**".

3) This idea **links Daisy** to the **mythological Sirens**. The Sirens sang **irresistible** songs, causing sailors to **throw themselves** into the **sea** and **drown**. **Metaphorically**, Gatsby **drowns** trying to reach Daisy across the **Sound**.

4) Daisy is repeatedly **linked** with **light**. She behaves "**radiantly**" and has a "**glowing face**", with "**bright eyes and a bright passionate mouth**". The **origin** of 'Daisy' is '**day's eye**' which could suggest that she **glows** like the **sun**.

5) Gatsby's **obsessed** with Daisy because she **symbolises everything** that he **wants**, but he also has **genuinely loves** her because she's:

- **capable** of **real affection** — she seems **genuinely fond** of **Nick** and **sincerely loves Gatsby**.
- a bit of a **naïve dreamer** who **idealises** their **past relationship** and believes they can **re-create** it — she carries "**well-forgotten dreams from age to age**".

...but she can't *Live Up* to *Gatsby's Dream*

1) Gatsby **idealises Daisy** and **never realises** she's **unworthy** of his **dreams** — **love** has **blinded him** to her **flaws**.

2) For all her **good qualities**, Daisy is also **materialistic** and **self-absorbed**. Her **affection** for **others** never overcomes her **selfishness**, so she seems **disloyal**. E.g. she stays with Tom because he can give her **security**, regardless of how this affects Gatsby. She also **disappears** without a word, letting Gatsby take the **blame** for Myrtle's death.

3) Beneath her **attractive appearance**, Daisy's **shallow** and **empty**. Her voice is **appealing**, but she **never** says anything **insightful** — her use of **short questions, hyperbole** and **pointless stories** indicates a **lack of depth**.

4) It's suggested that she murmurs **deliberately** "**to make people lean toward her**". This gives the impression that the **attractive power** of her voice is just a **meaningless trick** that she uses to **manipulate** people.

5) Daisy wants, and is **used to**, a **life of privilege** — she's **scared of change**. She seems **more interested** in Gatsby's **possessions** than **Gatsby himself**: "**It makes me sad because I've never seen... such beautiful shirts before**".

In **Nick's opinion**, Daisy could never **live up** to Gatsby's **expectations** because of the "**colossal vitality of his illusion**". After being **reunited** with her, even Gatsby is **disappointed** at times: "**I feel far away from her**".

Daisy Buchanan

Daisy is *Easily Controlled by Men*

1) Daisy **tends** to be **guided** by the other **characters** — she lets both Tom and Gatsby **dictate** to her, and she is easily **persuaded** to marry Tom.

2) Daisy stays with Tom because he's **all she knows** and he's the strongest personality in the novel. She can't **give up** her **life** to be **with Gatsby** no matter how **unhappy** she is — she's a **dreamer**, but she isn't brave enough to **break free** of **society's expectations**.

3) In the hotel scene, where **Daisy decides** to stay with Tom, she **says** very **little**. **Tom dominates** the conversation, **bullying** and **bossing** her about — this proves that his character's more **powerful** than **Daisy** or **Gatsby**.

4) Nick describes her voice as a **"deathless song"** and yet she **can't speak** when Tom and Gatsby, two **strong male personalities**, are **fighting over her**. This emphasises her **weakness** and **inability** to make her **own decisions**.

5) It could be argued that Daisy **realises** how **little control** she has over her life. She thinks that a **beautiful fool** is **"the best thing a girl can be"** — a **beautiful** girl will be able to **attract** a **rich husband**, and a fool won't **notice** or **care** if her husband **controls her** and **cheats** on her.

> Daisy always wears white. White is an absence of colour, so Fitzgerald could be implying that metaphorically she's a blank canvas that can be manipulated in any way that the other characters want.

She's an *Ambiguous Character*

1) Fitzgerald makes it **ambiguous** whether Daisy is a **weak victim** who should be **pitied**, or if she's **deliberately manipulative**. This ambiguity is **obvious** in her **maiden name "Fay"** — 'Fay' is an **old English word** for 'fairy', but it also **links her** to **Morgan le Fay**, a **legendary evil sorceress** who tried to overthrow King Arthur.

2) All the **textual evidence** is open to a range of **different interpretations**, for example:

- She marries Tom instead of waiting for Gatsby:

  | Society **wouldn't allow** her to be **with Gatsby**, but **approved** of Tom as a **husband**. | OR | She chose Tom because she was **materialistic** and **cared** about **money** more than she cared about Gatsby. |

- She cries at the sight of Gatsby's expensive shirts:

  | She's **shallow** and **materialistic** and is **only attracted** to **Gatsby** because of his **expensive lifestyle**. | OR | She **cries** because she is **overwhelmed** by the **situation**. |

- She allows Gatsby to take the blame for Myrtle's death:

  | It was Gatsby's idea in the first place — she's just a **weak character** who **gives** in to the **strongest personality**. | OR | She's **selfish** and **cowardly**, and doesn't **appreciate** Gatsby's sacrifice. |

3) Although Nick seems to be **attracted** to Daisy, it's also clear from the start that he feels some **resentment** towards her. He describes her smile as a **"smirk"** and thinks she has **"asserted her membership"** of a **"distinguished secret society"**.

4) However, Nick's **portrayal** of Daisy may be **biased** — he obviously feels **bitter** towards Daisy after **Gatsby's death**. For example, although he claims to feel no **"resentment"** towards her, he's clearly angry that she hasn't **"sent a message or a flower"** and later reflects on her **"vast carelessness"**.

Practice Questions

Q1 Analyse Fitzgerald's presentation of Daisy's character throughout *The Great Gatsby*. Do you think she comes across as more of a victim or a villain? Back up your answer with examples from the text.

Q2 'The name Daisy suggests that she's pretty, delicate but ultimately fairly common — there's nothing very special about her.' To what extent do you agree with this statement? Refer to the text in your answer.

"High in a white palace, the king's daughter, the golden girl..."

Daisy's looks are ambiguous, as well as her personality. It's never exactly clear what colour her hair is. Nick says it's "dark" and "blue"; Daisy describes her daughter's hair as "yellowy" and then says "she's got my hair". But in films, for some reason, she's usually blonde.

Tom Buchanan

What Tom wants, Tom gets — and he doesn't care what he has to do to get it... Unfortunately this means that he isn't the nicest of men. He's also a snob, a sexist and a racist to boot. Daisy's one lucky lady.

He's **Selfish** and **Does What he Wants**

© PARAMOUNT / THE KOBAL COLLECTION

1) Tom is **married** to Daisy, but he's had a **string** of **affairs**.

2) He **selfishly** pursues his **desires** with **no regard** for the **consequences**. His **infidelities** are a good example — he had a **"little spree"** in Chicago, an **affair** with a chambermaid just after his **honeymoon**, and Myrtle is just the **latest** of his **mistresses**.

3) At Yale, Tom was **"one of the most powerful ends that ever played football"** — his sporting **success** at **college** makes everything else feel like an **"anti-climax"**.

4) Because Tom is 'old money', and his **wealth** was **inherited**, he feels like he's **better** than **everyone else** — he **spends money freely** and **treats** other people **badly** to **prove it**.

5) Tom does have some **redeeming features** — he seems to have **genuine feelings** for both **Myrtle** and **Daisy**. When he **discovers** Myrtle's **dead** his **"tears were overflowing"**, and when Daisy **tells him** she **doesn't love him** he **pleads** with **"a husky tenderness"**.

Tom is **Physical** and likes to be in **Control**

1) **Descriptions** of Tom **focus** on his **physicality** — Daisy describes him as **"great, big, hulking"** and a **"brute"**. Tom's **appearance** is **linked** to his **physical behaviour** and his need to be in **control** at all times. His clothes can't hide his **"cruel body"**, just as his **sophistication** and **money** can't hide his **brutal nature**.

2) Tom is **cold** and **rude** to demonstrate his **superiority** over **others**. When he's buying Myrtle's dog, he **challenges** the salesman, **"That's no police dog"**, and then **overrules** him, **"'It's a bitch,' said Tom decisively"**.

3) In this **exchange** Tom also shows a **disregard** for **money** which lets him **dominate** the lower classes. When he says **"Here's your money. Go and buy ten more dogs"**, Tom simultaneously **insults** the salesman by implying he's **dishonestly overpriced** the dog, while showing that he's **so rich** it doesn't **matter** to him **how much** the dog costs.

4) Tom's **language** also shows that he likes to be in control — he **regularly** uses the personal **pronoun "I"**, for example, telling Nick **"I've got a nice place here"** rather than 'We've', which **excludes** Daisy from his **achievements**.

He's also a **Bully**

Tom's only physically abusive to women, which could suggest that he's a coward, or that he sees them as his property.

1) Tom **bullies people** both **verbally** and **physically**:

VERBALLY

- Tom **silences** any **opposition** by **interrupting** and **talking over** other people — in his **first appearance**, he **interrupts** both **Daisy** and **Jordan** so he can **make his point**. Even though Tom's **upper class** and **knows** how to **act politely**, he **doesn't care**.

- Tom uses **orders** to **control people** — he ends his **first conversation** with Nick by turning Nick around **"politely and abruptly"** and **telling** him **"We'll go inside"**.

- He uses **verbal assaults** to **persuade** Daisy to **stay with him** in **Chapter 7**. His **attack** on Gatsby makes Daisy **withdraw into herself** and beg him **"*Please*, Tom! I can't stand this any more"**.

PHYSICALLY

- When **verbal** assaults **don't work**, Tom **resorts** to **violence**. When Myrtle **doesn't respond** to his **verbal threats** in **Chapter 2** (see p.9) he **breaks her nose** without even **thinking**.

- Tom doesn't **physically** abuse Daisy, but accidentally **bruises** her **finger** — he's not **in control** of his **strength**.

- It's **suggested** that he even **enjoys violence** — he's **excited** by the **thought** of a **"wreck"** in **Chapter 7** (see p.19).

2) Tom **thinks** that the **best way** to **deal** with **problems** is to **confront them directly** — this is how he **wins** Daisy back. By **forcing** a **confrontation** with Gatsby he **regains control** of the **situation** and his **wife**.

3) He's also **vindictive** — after he's **ended Gatsby's dream** of **reuniting** with Daisy he makes them **travel home together**, just to **rub salt** in Gatsby's **wounds**. He **knows** that Gatsby's **no longer** a **threat** to him.

Tom Buchanan

He Represents the Immorality and Materialism of the 'Jazz Age'

1) Fitzgerald thought that the 'Jazz Age' was **hypocritical** and this is **reflected** by Tom's **behaviour**:

- He's **appalled** when he learns of **Daisy's affair** with Gatsby, but he has **lots of affairs** himself.
- He **criticises Gatsby** for "sneering at family life", but "was God knows where" when his daughter was born.
- He also **criticises** Gatsby for **knowing criminals** and for being a **bootlegger**, but Tom also knows criminals and he likes to **drink**, which shows that he **doesn't follow** the **prohibition laws** either.
- He sets a **high moral standard** for **other people**, such as Gatsby, but has **no morals** himself. Nick notes that he moves "from libertine to prig" to suit his needs.

2) Tom's **wealth** and **sense of superiority** makes him "careless" and **uncaring**. Nick **summarises** Tom and Daisy's **behaviour** when he says "they smashed up things and creatures and then retreated back into their money... and let other people clean up the mess...". They **run away** from their **problems** and never face the **consequences**.

3) He acts as a **foil** to **Gatsby** — Gatsby is **loyal**, **sensitive** and **caring** whilst Tom is more or less the **opposite**. For example, he only seems to **start caring** for Daisy when he sees he could **lose her**. This suggests his reaction is as much about **pride** and **possessiveness** as about actually **caring** for her. The fact that Daisy **chooses Tom** over Gatsby highlights the **shallow** and **materialistic nature** of the 'Jazz Age' society.

4) Like Daisy, Tom is **materialistic** — he has to **appear** to have the **best** of **everything**. For example, he was married with "more pomp and circumstance than Louisville ever knew".

He's Prejudiced and Not very Bright

1) Tom is a **racist** who worries that immigrants will challenge his **privileged existence**. He fears that "the white race will be... utterly submerged" and that society will one day allow "intermarriage between black and white".

2) Tom's **racism** could be a **front** for his **fear** that the 'new rich' will **take over**. He's "old-fashioned" which means he's **old-money aristocracy** and **likes** the **traditional class system** where he's **on top**.

3) He's **scared** of **anything** that **threatens** his **superiority** — he seems **more upset** that Daisy's having an affair with "Mr. Nobody from Nowhere" than that she's having an **affair** at all.

4) He's also a **sexist** who feels **threatened** by **independent women** — he doesn't like **Jordan** and **Daisy** having **freedom**, saying "women run around too much these days".

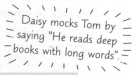

Daisy mocks Tom by saying "He reads deep books with long words".

5) **Ironically**, Tom seems to be fairly **well-read** and he places **great importance** on **science** even though he **doesn't understand** what he's read. He isn't very **clever**, and whenever he tries to justify his prejudices he's **hesitant** and **speaks** in **rambling half sentences**:

- In **Chapter 1**, he gives a **nonsensical** explanation of why "civilization's going to pieces". He explains "we're Nordics. I am, and you are and you are, and... And we've produced all the things that go to make civilization — oh, science and art and all that. Do you see?" (see p.7).
- Tom is **insecure** about his **lack of intelligence**: "'You think I'm pretty dumb, don't you?... Perhaps I am, but I have a — almost a second sight... Maybe you don't believe that, but science — '".

Practice Questions

Q1 When Fitzgerald considered Daisy's response to the accusations that Tom levels at Gatsby in Chapter 7 he wrote that "I can't quite place Daisy's reaction." Suggest reasons why Daisy returned to Tom and assess whether they are realistic.

Q2 'Although Tom is the least likeable character in the novel, he's also the most honest character.' Decide whether this is a fair assessment of Tom in comparison with the other characters in the novel.

Q3 Analyse the similarities and differences between Tom and Gatsby. To what extent is Tom a foil to Gatsby?

"... a brute of a man, a great, big, hulking physical specimen..."

Just some of the words used to describe this horribly violent man. He almost sounds like a superhero — apart from the casual racism. Using his polo skills as a force for good and not evil, Buchanaman triumphs over the downtrodden working classes. Hooray!

George and Myrtle Wilson

Georgie Porgie, pudding and pie, kissed the girls and made them cry, when the boys came out to play, he locked up his wife and then watched her get killed in a brutal hit and run accident. Ah — the nursery rhymes of my childhood...

The **Wilsons** have an **Unhappy Marriage**

1) George seems to be **besotted** with his wife, but Myrtle is **disgusted** by her husband and **treats him** "**as if he were a ghost**".

2) Their **marriage** is **unhappy** because:

© PARAMOUNT / THE KOBAL COLLECTION

   - They're **poor** and **business isn't good**.
   - Myrtle wants a strong, dominant man. She tells George to "**Throw me down and beat me, you dirty little coward!**".
   - Myrtle thinks George is **below** her **socially**, and she **treats him** as such.

3) The Wilsons are the only **major characters** to live near the **valley of ashes**, and they provide the **only glimpse** for the reader into the **lives** of the **working classes**.

4) They're **both victims** of **upper-class carelessness**:

   - **Tom** gives George and Myrtle **hope** that they can **escape poverty** — he promises to **sell** George a **car**, and he **allows** Myrtle to **believe** he wants to **marry her**, but he seems to have **no intention** of doing either.
   - Daisy's **reckless driving** kills Myrtle, and George **kills himself** through **grief**.

Myrtle **Aspires** to a **Better Life**

> Myrtle is the only thing associated with the valley of ashes which isn't covered in dust — this symbolises her lust for life.

1) To **heighten** the **tragedy** of Myrtle's **death**, Nick **emphasises** her **hunger for life**, frequently using the word "**vitality**" to **describe** her. She has a "**vitality about her as if the nerves of her body were continually smouldering.**"

2) Myrtle **resents** George because he isn't **rich** — he even had to **borrow** "**somebody's best suit to get married in**".

3) Myrtle **thinks** she married **below her class**, she says George "**wasn't fit to lick my shoe**", but she's actually **working class** herself. This is clear from the way she **speaks** — she uses **non-standard grammar** and "**obscene**" language.

4) Nick **ridicules** Myrtle's attempts to **appear upper class** — he describes her voice as a "**high mincing shout**". This **lack** of **sympathy** encourages the reader to see Myrtle as **greedy**, rather than **ambitious** or **desperate**.

5) She **naively** thinks that Tom will **leave** Daisy and clings to him despite his **abuse**, because he's **rich** and **upper class**.

> **Myrtle's name**
>
> Like Daisy, **Myrtle** is **named after** a **plant** — myrtle is a **shrub**. This may imply that Myrtle's intended as a **foil** to Daisy. The myrtle plant was sacred to Aphrodite, goddess of **love** and **sexuality**. Fitzgerald's descriptions **sexualise** Myrtle — e.g. "**sensuously**" and "**wet her lips**" — which **emphasises** that her **relationship** with Tom is based on **sex**. This contrasts with Tom and **Daisy's** relationship, which is based on **money** and **class**.

George is a **Weak Victim**

1) **Unlike** most other characters, George is presented as **loyal**, **selfless** and **hard-working**. He's presented **sympathetically** as a **victim** of the **selfish materialism** in the East.

2) George is a **foil** to Tom — George is **weak**, **passive** and is **easily manipulated**, whereas Tom is **strong** and **controlling**. George is **responsible** for Gatsby's **death**, but it's clear that **Tom used him** to "**clean up**" his "**mess**".

3) George isn't very **bright** — he seems **oblivious** to his wife's **affair** and to the **chemistry** between Myrtle and Tom.

4) It's **unclear** why George **commits suicide** — he could feel **responsible** for Myrtle's death or perhaps thinks that **life** isn't **worth living** without her: "**He was his wife's man and not his own**".

5) George is the **only character** to **talk about God** — this emphasises the lack of **religious morality** in **society**.

6) The other characters rarely seem to consider the **morality** of their **actions**, but George thinks God **sees everything**: "**You may fool me but you can't fool God!**" He **doesn't realise** that he's just looking at an **advertising billboard**. This shows that **religion** has been **replaced** by the **worship** of **material goods** (see p.42).

Jordan Baker

For a bit of a change I thought I'd let you write your own punch line — Why does Jordan make a good baker?
Because she .... I wrote my own but it was considered too rude to print.

Jordan is **Dishonest** and **Cynical**

1) Jordan is a **well-known professional golfer**, so she's a **target** for **gossip** — there was a "**scandal**" about her **cheating** in her **first golf tournament**.

2) Her only family is an **aunt** who's "**about a thousand years old**", so she's had to **learn** to **look after herself**. This has made her **hard** and **cynical** about life.

3) She's **dishonest** and **frequently lies** to get **what she wants** or to **avoid trouble** — she **denied** having "**left a borrowed car out in the rain with the top down**".

4) She's **practical**, as shown by the fact that she helped Daisy to **sober up** so she could attend her "**bridal dinner**", but she's also a **romantic** — she **encourages Nick** to help Gatsby and Daisy have an **affair**.

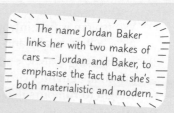

The name Jordan Baker links her with two makes of cars — Jordan and Baker, to emphasise the fact that she's both materialistic and modern.

She **Avoids Emotional Connections**

1) Jordan **distances herself** to avoid **getting hurt** or **found out**:

> Some critics argue that Jordan's gay because of Fitzgerald's masculine description of her "erect carriage" and "hard jaunty body". This more likely symbolises that she's rejected the role of a submissive woman expected by previous generations.

- She looks as if she's balancing an "**invisible but absorbing object on the tip of her chin**" — this suggests that she's **pretending** to be **aloof**, and **not part** of the **conversations** going on around her.

- She tries to **defuse conflict** by making **jokes** — for example when things are **building** to a **climax** in the hotel, Jordan "**respectfully**" whispers "**It's a swell suite**".

- She "**instinctively avoided clever shrewd men**" because she **doesn't want** to be **challenged**.

2) It's only when Jordan's with Nick that she lets her **guard down** and **reveals** something of her **true self**. Twice in the novel she **indicates** that she has **genuine feelings** for Nick — after Myrtle's **death** she **asks** Nick **inside twice**, but he **rejects** her. When Jordan **phones** Nick at work she **admits** she **wants** to **see him**, but he **refuses**.

3) When she **realises** that Nick's just as **careless** as **everyone else** Jordan **rejects** her **feelings** for him and says "**I don't give a damn about you now**". She **denies** being **hurt** by his **rejection**, saying she only felt "**a little dizzy**".

She provides a **Comparison** with **Daisy**

1) **Unlike Daisy**, Jordan is very **independent** — men expect her to "**yield**" but she doesn't **give in** to their **expectations**.

2) Jordan doesn't **say much** and seems to **consider** her **words carefully**, whereas Daisy **chats inanely**. She's **direct** and **assertive** to **emphasise** her **independence**, e.g. "**Don't talk.**" and "**Listen, Tom.**" She uses **statements** instead of **questions** to take **control** of **conversations**: "**You live in West Egg**".

3) While Daisy's **stuck in the past**, Jordan is "**too wise ever to carry well-forgotten dreams from age to age.**" This suggests that Jordan **looks forward** instead of **back** — she's **practical** and **moves on** from the **past**. It also hints at a **tired cynicism** — she doesn't **hope** and **dream**, because she **expects** to be **disappointed**.

4) However, Jordan is part of the same "**careless**" **upper-class** world as Daisy — she **acknowledges** that she's a "**bad driver**" (a **careless** person) but **chooses not to change**. This is partly why Nick **ends** their **relationship**.

Practice Questions

Q1 In what ways do Myrtle and George change according to the various settings that they occupy in the novel? Give examples from the text to support your answer.

Q2 'Jordan Baker is the only likeable character because she's the only character who's aware of her own flaws'. To what extent do you agree with this statement? Refer to the text in your answer.

"She was incurably dishonest. She wasn't able to endure being at a disadvantage"

I'm incurably dishonest when it comes to playing poker. It's not the best tactic because everyone knows that I'm bluffing in every single hand. Except for when I'm bluffing that I'm bluffing. I've confused myself now... I don't know how Jordan does it.

Meyer Wolfshiem

At first glance Wolfshiem appears to be a fairly generic gangster, but as with all of the characters in 'The Great Gatsby' he's not all bad. Just mostly bad. He and Gatsby are supposedly friends, but there's no honour among thieves...

Wolfshiem Represents *the* Criminal Underworld *of the 1920s*

1) Wolfshiem is **first introduced** just **after** Gatsby has described his past life as a **"young rajah"** and claimed to have **inherited** his **money**.

2) **Juxtaposing** Gatsby's tall stories with his **connection** to Wolfshiem's obviously **criminal activities** strongly **hints** that Gatsby isn't all he **seems to be**. It adds weight to **rumours** that Gatsby's a **criminal** and **didn't inherit** his **money**.

3) Wolfshiem's character is **based on Arnold Rothstein** — a **notorious Jewish gangster** who lived in **New York** and was **involved** in **bootlegging**. Rothstein was **believed** to have **bribed** a baseball team to **deliberately lose** the World Series. In the novel, Gatsby claims that **Wolfshiem "fixed the World's Series"**.

4) Nick says that Wolfshiem **played** with **"the faith of fifty million people"**. Fitzgerald's use of the word **"faith"** links **gambling** with **religion**. This suggests that religion's been **replaced** by **materialism** and emphasises the idea that the pursuit of **wealth** has become the **main focus** of **American life**.

5) Wolfshiem's **connection** to Walter Chase, a **friend of Tom's**, shows **how far** the **criminal corruption** has **spread**.

Wolfshiem is an Ambiguous Character

His name makes him sound like a predator and suggests that he's ruthless.

1) Wolfshiem is an **odd mix** of **contradictory qualities**. He's **sentimental** but also **hard** and **businesslike**:

Sentimental

- Like **Dan Cody**, Wolfshiem is a **father figure** to Gatsby, and even **set him up** in **business**: **"Start him! I made him"**. Wolfshiem makes it **sound as if** he set Gatsby on an **honest path**, but he actually made him a **criminal**.

- Wolfshiem talks about **"friends gone now forever"**. He's clearly **emotional** and misses old friends — he's one of the **few characters** to **grieve** for Gatsby. He says they were **"always together"**, as his **"eyes filled with tears"**.

Businesslike

- His **language** is sometimes **aggressive** — **"don't pay him a penny till he shuts his mouth"**. He speaks in **orders** and **statements** instead of **questions**: **"I understand you're looking for a business gonnegtion"**.

- He **doesn't attend** Gatsby's **funeral** because he doesn't want to **"get mixed up"** with Gatsby's suspicious **death**.

- Wolfshiem's **influence** in Gatsby's **success** continues the **idea** that the **American Dream** has been **corrupted** — he teaches Gatsby that the **best way** for a **working-class** man to be successful is through **illegal activities**.

2) Wolfshiem's **behaviour** is a **mix** of **sentimentality** and **practicality** — he says it's better to **"show our friendship for a man when he is alive and not after he is dead"**.

3) His **appearance** is also **ambiguous** — Fitzgerald describes his eating habits using the **oxymoron "ferocious delicacy"**, and his **sophisticated manner** of **dress** is **offset** by the fact that his cuff-links are made from **human molars**.

He's a Caricature *of a* Jewish Criminal

1) Nick's **description** of Wolfshiem reveals both his **anti-Semitic prejudice** and his **willingness** to **judge people**.

2) Wolfshiem is presented as **short**, **showy** and involved in **underhand dealings** — a **common portrayal** of **Jews** in the **1920s**. Nick **draws attention** to Wolfshiem's **"tragic"** nose and **mocks** his **speech**: **"gonnegtion"** and **"Oggsford"**.

3) This makes Wolfshiem appear to be an almost **comic character**, which is **inappropriate** given his **ruthless behaviour**.

4) It could be argued that this **racist presentation** of Jews was **common** at the time, and Nick is simply **reflecting** a **general fear** and **ignorance** that **many Americans** had about **Jewish people**.

Other Characters

Dan's the man, at least in Gatsby's eyes. On a similar theme, I could say that Michaelis is the greatest, but it doesn't quite rhyme. Unless you say it really weirdly. Anyway, he's not all that great, so this was all a massive waste of time...

Dan Cody was a Father Figure to Gatsby

1) Gatsby **virtually disowned** his **mother** and **father** because "**his imagination had never really accepted them as his parents at all**". This is why Cody was so **influential** in **shaping Gatsby** into the **man** that he **became**.

2) Until the age of seventeen Gatsby was just **James Gatz** — Cody taught him how to be **Jay Gatsby**.

3) Gatsby **always dreamed** of something **bigger**, and Dan Cody **proved** that it was **possible**. Cody gave Gatsby his **first taste** of the **elite life** and the American Dream — Cody was a **self-made millionaire** with a **life** of "**lavish doings**".

4) Gatsby wanted to **achieve** the **same things** as Cody, but he also worked out how to **improve** on Cody's example:

- Cody had a **drink problem**, but Gatsby "**formed the habit of letting liquor alone**".
- Cody's behaviour was **debauched** — he indulged in "**the savage violence of the frontier brothel and saloon**". Gatsby throws **debauched parties** but he himself "**grew more correct as the fraternal hilarity increased**".

5) Nick says Cody had an "**empty face**" which could suggest that he was **unfulfilled** in spite of his **success**.

> Gatsby is more like his real father than he realises. Henry Gatz is also more concerned with illusions than reality — the photo of Gatsby's mansion is "more real... than the house itself."

Owl Eyes and Klipspringer are Representative of all Gatsby's Guests

1) **Owl Eyes** is a "**stout, middle-aged man**" who Nick meets at one of Gatsby's **parties**. Owl Eyes is **impressed** by the fact that Gatsby's books are "**absolutely real**" because he assumed that they'd be "**cardboard**" — this shows that **everyone suspects** that there's something **suspicious** about Gatsby.

2) Owl Eyes also points out that Gatsby "**didn't cut the pages**" — meaning he **hasn't read** them. This reinforces the idea that the **library** is just part of the **façade** that Gatsby **hides behind**.

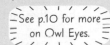
> See p.10 for more on Owl Eyes.

3) **Klipspringer** is known as the "**boarder**" because he spends **so much time** at Gatsby's **mansion** — he's just one of the **many guests** who turn up at Gatsby's parties **uninvited**.

4) Gatsby's **too polite** to **turn them away**, so they **take advantage** of his **hospitality**. But they don't **care** about him — of the "**hundreds**" of guests, **only Owl Eyes** attends his **funeral**, while Klipspringer is **more concerned** about his "**tennis shoes**", and misses the funeral for a "**picnic or something**". This **reflects** the **shallowness** and **selfishness** of the era.

5) Klipspringer is named after an **animal** (an antelope) as are many of the **guests** — e.g. "Leeches", "Beaver", "Ferret". Fitzgerald may be **playfully implying** that they **focus** on their **animal urges** and lack **humanity**.

Michaelis Witnesses the Novel's Climax

1) Michaelis is the "**young Greek**" who runs a "**coffee joint**" **next door** to the Wilson's **garage** — he's a fairly **two-dimensional character** who's presented simply as a **good neighbour** and a **reliable witness**.

2) His **main role** in the novel is to **provide evidence** for the **investigation** of Myrtle's **death**, and Fitzgerald uses him as a **narrative device** to provide a **first-hand account** of the **events** where Nick isn't **present**.

3) The **upper-class characters** leave Wilson **alone** and focus on **their own problems**, but Michaelis **remains**. His caring behaviour highlights the **selfishness** of the other characters.

Practice Questions

Q1 Using Nick's portrayal of Wolfshiem as a starting point, assess how Fitzgerald presents attitudes to race in *The Great Gatsby*.

Q2 "Even without the influence of Cody and Wolfshiem, Gatsby's personality would have resulted in him achieving the same wealth and success." To what extent do you agree with this statement? Refer to the text in your answer.

"...a grey, florid man with a hard empty face — the pioneer debauchee"

Dan Cody, Klipspringer and Michaelis — so much more than just filler for a spare page. No, seriously. They are. Well, Michaelis not so much, but definitely Dan Cody. Without Cody, Gatsby might have turned out completely differently, and then there'd be no book at all...

Money and the American Dream

If 'The Great Gatsby' were a fancy dress theme, everyone would turn up looking extravagantly glamorous but empty of hope, morals or a sense of purpose. Sounds like my typical Friday night — except without the extravagant glamour...

There is a **Big Gap** between the **Rich** and the **Poor**

1) Most of the characters in the novel are **very wealthy** and live a **life** of **luxury**. The **rich** and **glamorous atmosphere** defines the novel's **tone** — the focus on the **upper-class lifestyle** gives the **novel** a **mood** of **lively extravagance**. E.g. Gatsby owns a beach, motor-boats and a Rolls-Royce and his parties are full of "**faces and voices and colour**".

2) However, this society is **contrasted** with the **poverty** of those living near to the **valley of ashes**. The **location** of the **valley of ashes** between the **wealthy Egg communities** and **New York** makes the **contrast stronger**.

3) There is also a **constant sense** that the **glamorous lives** of the upper classes are **essentially meaningless**:

   - **Beneath** the surface, everyone is **bored** because they have **no purpose** — Daisy seems to realise this when she asks what they should do "**this afternoon... and the day after that, and the next thirty years?**".

   - Many friendships appear **superficial** e.g. Gatsby's parties are full of "**enthusiastic meetings between women who never knew each other's names**". This shows that the society is full of **pretence** and **loneliness**.

   - Many of Gatsby's guests had **tragic fates**, e.g. "**drowned**", "**strangled his wife**", "**killed himself**". This reinforces the message that behind the **lighthearted partying**, much of society was **deeply unhappy**.

4) Fitzgerald's portrayal invites the reader to be **critical** of the characters' **empty**, **materialistic** lives while **simultaneously** making those lives seem **exciting** and **beautiful**. This reflects his **own attitude** towards **wealth**.

Characters have Different Attitudes to Money

1) The characters are **defined** by their **relationship with money** — it affects how they **act**, how they **see themselves** and how **others see** them:

   - **Nick** is **confused** about how to **respond** to wealth and decadence. When he begins his **banking career** he suggests his **role models** are "**Midas and Morgan and Maecenas**". At the same time Nick says that **Gatsby's empty display** of **wealth**, "**represented everything for which I have an unaffected scorn**".

     > *Midas is a legendary king whose touch turned things to solid gold. Morgan was one of the most successful bankers of the 19th century. Maecenas was a very wealthy patron of the arts in Ancient Rome.*

   - **Daisy and Tom** take their wealth **for granted**. Tom assumes it is his **natural right** to be at the **top** of society, and Daisy was "**casual**" about the beautiful house she grew up in. This attitude makes them "**careless people**" — they never worry when they hurt other people, they can **retreat** "**back into their money**".

   - **Gatsby** used to be "**extravagantly ambitious**" and **focused** on **financial gain**. However, the **Gatsby** that Nick meets doesn't get **involved** in the **decadence** of his own parties. This suggests that he has grown to be **indifferent** to his wealth — he just sees it as a **means** towards **winning Daisy**.

   - For **Myrtle**, **money buys happiness** — she gets pleasure from her **cold cream**, **pet dog** and **magazines**. Her **opinion** of her **husband** was **damaged** by the realisation that he **couldn't afford** to buy a **suit** for their **wedding**.

2) Money takes on a **meaning beyond** its **financial worth**. For Gatsby, **money** is **confused** with **love**. He says **Daisy's voice** is "**full of money**", linking his **longing** for **her** with his **longing** for the **wealth** and **status** that she **represents**.

Money Causes a Social Divide

1) The people who live in **East Egg** come from **old**, **wealthy families** and have **inherited** money. They see themselves as **elegant** and **well-mannered**.

2) **West Egg** is the home of the '**new money**' — **people** who have **recently** made their money through **business**.

3) The people of East Egg **look down** on the people who live in West Egg because they consider their **family backgrounds** to be '**inferior**' and their **ostentatious displays** of wealth to be in **bad taste** (see p.6).

4) Gatsby realises that **money** isn't enough to **cross** the **social divide** between himself and Daisy — he needs to be **upper class** to be seen as **her equal**. His **affected speech** and **imported shirts** are an attempt to **imitate** the upper classes.

Money and the American Dream

The **American Dream** was corrupted by **Greed**

1) The United States **Declaration of Independence** says that every citizen has the right to "**Life**, **Liberty** and the pursuit of **Happiness**". This is seen by **many** to **express** the essential spirit of the **American Dream**:

> **The American Dream**
> Any **individual** should be able to achieve **success** through their own **ambition** and **hard work**, without being **held back** by their social **class** or **family** background.

2) The **American Dream** is about people having the **opportunity** to **succeed**, it's not just about **money** or **possessions**. During the **1920s** the dream of freedom and success was **replaced** with the **dream of money**.

3) During the **post-war economic boom** (see p.56) **anyone** could try to become **wealthy**. However, the novel highlights the clear **class barriers** between 'old' money and 'new' money which show that America follows the same **strict social hierarchy** that the **American Dream** hoped to **avoid**.

4) This suggests the American Dream became **corrupted**, which is the **main theme** of the novel.

Gatsby represents the **American Dream**

1) Gatsby is literally a **self-made** man — he **invented** himself. Gatsby's character **embodies** the American Dream — his **entire identity**, as well as his wealth, was achieved through **hope**, **hard work** and **ambition**.

2) As a **young boy** he dreamed of being **great** — his father thought he would help "**build up the country**" and Gatsby set out a **strict schedule** focused on "**improving his mind**" and body. This **idea** of **self-improvement** is **central** to the **American Dream**.

3) When Gatsby meets Daisy, his **dream** of being a "**great man**" becomes a dream of being **wealthy** enough to **marry** her. This reflects the way the **American Dream** was corrupted to become the **pursuit** of **wealth**. Daisy is even described in **materialistic** terms, emphasising her status as a **symbol** of **wealth**:

> Daisy is described as "**gleaming like silver**" — she appears to **embody** the phrase '**made of money**'. Many men **loved** her which "**increased her value**" — this makes her sound like an **item** that is in **high demand**.

4) By narrowing his **ambitions** to **winning Daisy**, Nick thinks that Gatsby **limits** his potential: "**his mind would never romp again like the mind of God**". This is **similar** to the corruption of the **American Dream**, because it became about **obtaining wealth** rather than doing **great things**.

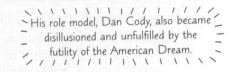
His role model, Dan Cody, also became disillusioned and unfulfilled by the futility of the American Dream.

> **The Trap of the American Dream**
> The American Dream **promotes** the **idea** that anyone can **achieve** their **ambitions** through **hard work**, regardless of their background, but the characters in *The Great Gatsby* **fail** to **overcome** the **barriers** of **class**. Gatsby will never '**earn**' upper-class status through hard work and **material possessions**. This implies that people are **judged** on **class** rather than **merit**, so the **American Dream** is **unattainable**.

Practice Questions

Q1 'If Gatsby had successfully won back Daisy, then he would have finally achieved the American Dream.' To what extent do you agree with this statement? Refer to the text in your answer.

Q2 Explain how Fitzgerald uses the characters of Daisy and Tom to explore the corruption of the American Dream. Consider how they view their own wealth and how they behave towards other people.

Q3 How do you think Nick's class and level of wealth affect him as a narrator?

"what preyed on Gatsby, what foul dust floated in the wake of his dreams"

Poor Gatsby. All he wanted was the woman of his dreams, but he got tangled up in the giddy materialism of the Roaring Twenties — followed around by the foul dust of Rolls-Royces, motor-boats, beautiful dresses and many cocktails — poor, dusty Gatsby.

Love and Relationships

'The Great Gatsby' is full of bright young things living the high life — but they don't seem very happy. Fitzgerald suggests it's because they're too greedy and selfish to be nice to each other. I think they just need more naps and cuddles...

Fitzgerald portrays **Different Kinds** of **Love**

1) In *The Great Gatsby* everyone's **seeking** to **form** and **keep romantic relationships** — they want to **love** and **be loved**.

2) However, this doesn't mean they're all looking for the **same thing**. Each character seems to view '**love**' in a completely **different** way which makes the **network** of relationships **complex**.

3) Lots of the **relationships** are **ambiguous** and **contain elements** of **different types** of **love**, but this **diagram** shows some of the **main types** of love between the **different characters**:

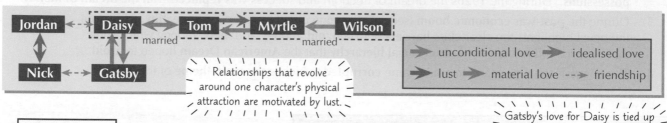

Relationships that revolve around one character's physical attraction are motivated by lust.

Gatsby's love for Daisy is tied up with his love of wealth, so in some ways his love for her is material.

Idealised Love

* Gatsby's **obsession** with Daisy has **transformed** his **memory** of her into an **image** of **perfection**. There's **no way** Daisy can live up to **Gatsby's imagined ideal**.

* Daisy's love for Gatsby could also be **idealised** — she claims to **love Gatsby**, but she's also **holding** on to the **past** and has **idealised** their **romance**. She could just be **in love** with the **feeling** of **being adored**.

Unconditional Love

* When Wilson **discovers Myrtle's affair** he's **crushed** and appears "**physically sick**" but he **still loves** her — her **death affects him** to the point where he starts to **act** "**sort of crazy**" and is **willing** to **commit murder**.

* Daisy and Tom's relationship has **elements** that seem **unconditional**. Tom appeals to Daisy to **remember** the day at the Punch Bowl with a "**husky tenderness**" that suggests there's **real affection** between them.

Material Love

* Myrtle **loves Tom** because of the **life** he represents and the **happiness** she gets from the **things** he **buys her**.

* But Myrtle's **materialism** affects her **marriage**. She "**can't stand**" Wilson, simply because he's **poor** and she regards him as a **failure**. Her **reaction** to the fact that he "**borrowed somebody's best suit**" for their wedding shows that her **feelings** are strongly **connected** to wealth — she "**lay down and cried**".

* To a **certain degree**, Tom and Daisy's **relationship** is held **together** by **material love** — **wealth** and **class** play a **big role**. Their **marriage** makes them **more respectable** in **society**, and they **need** each other to help **get** what they **want** in life — for Tom, Daisy's **beauty** makes her a **status symbol** and for Daisy, Tom offers **stability**.

Relationships are a source of *Conflict*

1) Most of the **relationships** in *The Great Gatsby* are **unhappy**, **unstable** or **violent** — this idea is hinted at **early** in the novel when two men **literally** remove their wives from Gatsby's garden by **brute force**: "**both wives were lifted, kicking, into the night**". The word "**kicking**" hints at the **violence** to come.

2) Men treat women as **possessions** and think they can do what they like with them — Tom gives **Myrtle** a **dog leash** which **symbolises** the fact that he's **in control** of the **affair**. Tom **decides** when they **see each other**, and even what **Myrtle** is allowed to **say** — he "**broke her nose with his open hand**" for daring to **say** his **wife's name**.

3) **Tom** and **Gatsby** also **argue** over Daisy as if she's a **possession** and they can **decide** who **keeps her**.

4) Fitzgerald **portrays love** as **violent** and **destructive** — all of the **marriages** in the novel are **unhappy**. This **dissatisfaction** with love escalates into **violence** and eventually **three characters die** — Myrtle, Gatsby and Wilson.

5) This could **reflect** Fitzgerald's own **dissatisfaction** and **unhappiness** with his **marriage** to Zelda. Fitzgerald and his wife had a **passionate relationship** filled with **tension**.

Love and Relationships

Friendships tend to be Shallow

1) Gatsby is **generous**, **hospitable** and **kind**, but in the end he's **abandoned** by all his acquaintances — "**Nobody came**" to his funeral except for Nick, his father, Owl Eyes, a few servants and the postman.

2) Gatsby **holds parties** and **forms bonds solely** to **find out** if anyone **knows Daisy** — he strikes up a **friendship with Nick** to **get access** to **Daisy**. Gatsby doesn't **trust anyone** with the **truth** about his **life** because he's **worried** about **preserving** his **carefully constructed persona**. He only tells Nick the **truth** once his persona has "**broken up like glass**".

3) Nick is Gatsby's most **loyal friend**, but even he isn't always **kind** or **complimentary** about Gatsby — **immediately after** he tells Gatsby "**You're worth the whole damn bunch put together**" he **admits** that he "**disapproved of him from beginning to end**" and this was "**the only compliment**" he ever gave him.

4) Wolfshiem also seems to **genuinely care** for Gatsby, they were "**always together**" and Nick calls him Gatsby's "**closest friend**", but he **refuses** to get "**mixed up**" with Gatsby's **death** and **funeral**.

5) This **failure** to make **successful relationships** with others **emphasises** Gatsby's **role** as an **isolated dreamer**. It also **reinforces** the **impression** that **everyone is isolated** and **nobody** really **understands anyone else**.

The Traditional Family Structure doesn't Exist in the novel

1) There are several **parents** mentioned, but none of them act as **strong role models** or give advice. They're all **distant** or **vague** figures who aren't **actively involved** in their children's lives:

   - Myrtle's mother is just an unclear **photograph** that Nick mistakes for a "**hen sitting on a blurred rock**".

   - Daisy's **treatment** of her daughter **indicates** that she's **not interested** in **her** — when Nick asks about Pammy, Daisy looks at Nick "**absently**" and is **more interested** in talking about **herself** as a **mother**: "**let me tell you what I said when she was born**". To Daisy, Pammy is just **another object** to be **shown off** and then **taken away**, while Tom **never mentions** his daughter, and wasn't even at her **birth**.

   - Gatsby's father appears "**helpless**" and **childlike** — Gatsby even **bought** him a **house**, which is a **reversal** of the **traditional parent-child relationship**. He's so **impressed** by his son's **wealth** that he doesn't seem able to **grieve** for Gatsby's death **properly**, because his sadness is "**mixed with an awed pride**".

2) The lack of **strong parent figures** could suggest that the **characters lack guidance** and aren't concerned with **traditional family values**.

3) The one **exception** is the **relationship** between Nick and his father — Nick still bears his father's **advice** in mind:

> "Whenever you feel like **criticizing** anyone... just remember that all the people in this world haven't had **the advantages** that you've had."

4) **Nick** tries to follow his father's advice, which suggests that **traditional family** values are **important** to him. This sets him **apart** from the other characters and the **materialistic** society of the East.

Practice Questions

Q1 'There is no true love in *The Great Gatsby*. Instead, money is the pivotal force that binds characters together.' To what extent do you agree with this statement? Back up your answer with examples from the text.

Q2 Compare how Nick behaves towards Gatsby, Daisy and Tom. What do these friendships reveal about his character?

Q3 Fitzgerald once said of Zelda, his wife: "I love her and that's the beginning and end of everything." Explore whether Gatsby's dreams begin or end after he falls in love with Daisy.

"Your wife doesn't love you... She's never loved you. She loves me."

You could say 'The Great Gatsby' was a love story — it is about Gatsby's overwhelming love for Daisy. But somehow it just doesn't seem that romantic. Maybe because he stalks her to New York and secretly buys the house opposite her and her family. Creepy...

Appearance and Reality

Appearance and reality are all muddled up. Reality feels several steps away — like looking at a photo of a painting in a mirror. It doesn't help that it's narrated by a guy who thinks ceilings are wedding cakes and couches are balloons...

There's a **Difference** between how things **Appear** and how they **Really Are**

1) Many characters are **unable** or **unwilling** to **face reality**, and prefer to see only **appearances**:

   - To Gatsby, Daisy **appears perfect**, but her **actions** show that she's actually **shallow**, **disloyal** and **materialistic**.
   - Gatsby **imagines** that Daisy **hasn't changed** from the girl he fell in love with **five years** ago. In **reality** she's now a **wife** and **mother**, but Gatsby **refuses** to see this. He's **shocked** when he meets Daisy's child because he had never "**really believed in its existence**".
   - Wilson sees the **eyes** of **Dr T.J. Eckleburg** as the eyes of **God**, but the **reader** knows that they're **sightless** and just "**an advertisement**". Eckleburg's eyes just **take on** whatever **meaning** the **viewer** gives them.
   - Mr Gatz's photo of his son's house is "**more real to him now than the house itself**". This suggests he can only comprehend a **small**, **visual representation** of his son's wealth. The **reality** is **too huge** to handle.

2) Similarly, the '**Jazz Age**' **appears exciting** and **glamorous** on the **surface**, but **underneath** it's **rotten** and **corrupt**.

The **Narrator's** view of **Reality** is often **Confused** by **Appearances**

The **reader only knows** what Nick **reveals**, and his grasp of **reality** is **distorted** by how things **appear** to him. For example:

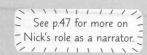
See p.47 for more on Nick's role as a narrator.

- In Chapter 1 Nick **over dramatises** the sound of the **phone ringing**, saying that his first instinct "**was to telephone immediately for the police**". In **reality**, all that's **happened** is that the **mood** of the **evening** has been **broken**.
- Nick believes that "**life is much more successfully looked at from a single window**" — this suggests that he could be **intentionally ignoring reality** for the sake of a **simpler picture**, so **not everything** he says can be **trusted**.
- Nick's **concerned** about what **other people think** — he wants to "**enter**" the lives of "**romantic women**", but doesn't want anyone to "**know or disapprove**". What people **see** is **more important** than what **really happens**.

By making a **character** in his story the narrator, Fitzgerald only provides a **partial viewpoint** of the events, where even the **narrator doesn't see** or **understand everything**. Nick's narration is **distorted**, but he **tries** to make his viewpoint **appear** to be **reality** — this adds more '**unreality**' to a novel already full of **superficiality**.

'**The Unreality of Reality**' is **Mirrored** in the **Physical World**

The **blurred line** between **fantasy** and **reality** extends to the **geography** and **weather** described in the novel:

Geography

- The valley of ashes is a "**fantastic**" place where "**ashes grow like wheat**" and **everything** is **made** of ash. The **name** also links it to the '**valley of the shadow of death**' — a metaphorical **image** of the world **derived** from the **Bible**.
- The Eggs are described as an "**arresting phenomenon**", a "**source of perpetual confusion**" and "**natural curiosities**" — these **descriptions** make them **sound unreal** and **cut off** from the rest of the world.

Weather

The weather **reflects** the **events** and **emotional tone** of the novel — this is called **pathetic fallacy**. E.g.

- Gatsby and Daisy's **disappointing** and **emotional** first meeting happens when it's "**pouring rain**".
- When their love is **rekindled**, the rain **stops** and the room is filled with "**twinkle-bells of sunshine**". This mirrors Gatsby's **change** in **emotion** — he "**literally glowed**" with happiness.

This makes events seem **unreal** because it suggests that **nature** is **mirroring** the characters' **emotions**.

Appearance and Reality

Most of the characters *Hide* behind **Disguises**

Just as the **glamorous life** of the East **masks** the **corruption underneath**, the characters also **hide** their **true identities**:

Gatsby is an *Illusion*

1) Gatsby is the **most important** example in the novel of a character who uses a **disguise** to hide his **true identity**.

2) Gatsby creates the **surface appearance** of inherited wealth and a distinguished history to hide the **reality** of his **impoverished past** and his **criminal present**. This allows him to pursue his **dream** of a **future** with Daisy.

3) It's clear that Gatsby's been **living a lie** for **years** — he originally dated Daisy "**under false pretences**".

- Gatsby is introduced through **gossip** — guests speculate that he once "**killed a man**", or was a "**spy**". Gatsby is a **mystery** — everyone **talks** about him but no one **knows** anything.

- People are **intrigued** by Gatsby's real identity, but in **trying** to **uncover** his past they just **add** to the **myth**. There are **hints** that people **suspect** that he's a **fake**, e.g. Owl Eyes is **amazed** that Gatsby's books are "**absolutely real**".

© PARAMOUNT / THE KOBAL COLLECTION

- Nick says that "**Jay Gatsby... sprang from his Platonic conception of himself**". **Plato**, a **Greek Philosopher**, **argued** that there was a **difference** between the **material world** which we **observe** and the **ideal world**. Nick **thinks** that Gatsby as a "**seventeen-year-old boy**" imagined an **ideal man**, and tried to make it a **reality**.

- Gatsby's **well developed persona** raises the **question** of **whether** an illusion can ever **become reality**.

Other Characters are also *Dishonest*

1) Nick suggests that "**personality is an unbroken series of successful gestures**". If this is true then it suggests that you can **control** the way that **people see you** and **be seen** as you **want** to **be seen**. Fitzgerald gives the impression of a **society** where **superficial appearances** are more important than **reality**:

- **Jordan** is "**incurably dishonest**" — Nick thinks she has to **pretend** to be someone she's not to **fit into** society. She has to appear "**cool, insolent**" but still wants to "**satisfy the demands of her hard, jaunty body**" — she wants **sexual freedom** but **without** the **labels** that come with it, so she's learnt to **lie**.

- **Myrtle's behaviour changes** according to **where** and **who she's with** — she tries to act upper class with Tom, referring to the servants as "**These people**" and saying that George "**wasn't fit to lick my shoe**". She's trying to **escape** the **reality** of the valley of ashes, and enter Tom's **privileged** society.

- **Daisy** and **Tom** try to keep up the **appearances** of a **happy marriage**, but **everyone knows** Tom's having an **affair**. Daisy **ignores reality** and the "**shrill metallic urgency**" of the telephone — she wants to **pretend** everything's **fine**.

2) It's **significant** that **all** of the characters who **attempt** to be **someone else** e.g. Gatsby and Myrtle, **fail** in the **end**.

Practice Questions

Q1 Both Nick and Gatsby have powerful imaginations that distort their views of reality. Discuss how this trait helps to develop their relationship and their characterisation.

Q2 Compare the importance of appearance and reality in the different social occasions that mark Gatsby's life — particularly his parties, interactions with business connections, and his funeral.

"a promise that the rock of the world was founded securely on a fairy's wing"

When Albert Einstein said "Imagination is more important than knowledge", he obviously hadn't read 'The Great Gatsby' — Nick's imagination makes it very hard to work out how much of the story is just happening in his head... I want cold, hard facts, man.

Religion and Morality

You wouldn't think there was much religion in 'The Great Gatsby' — those crazy cats with their affairs and selfishness and drunken shenanigans. But Fitzgerald uses religious references to reveal the emptiness beneath the glittering immorality.

The characters are Searching for New Values

1) **None** of the characters in the novel are **obviously religious** and they all seem to **lack religious morals**. Daisy **hits** and **kills** Myrtle but doesn't even **stop**, and Daisy, Tom and Myrtle all have **affairs**.

> After the First World War a 'lost generation' emerged, who felt that life was aimless and lacked morality (see p.56). People lost faith in religion and looked for other ways of coping.

2) The characters **rely** on **things** other than **religion** to guide their **actions**:

   - Tom **believes** in his own **racial** and **class superiority**. He worries that the **"white race"** will be **"utterly submerged"**. Nick comments that Tom's **immoral actions**, such as **causing Gatsby's death** were **"to him, entirely justified"**. Tom thinks that his **class protects him**, and his **status justifies** his **actions**.

   - Nick **follows** his **father's advice** — or at least tries to **bear it in mind**. He also **idolises** Gatsby's **"extraordinary gift for hope"**. His **faith in Gatsby** almost seems to stand in for a lack of **religious faith**: **"I had one of those renewals of complete faith in him that I'd experienced before"**.

   - Gatsby is **guided** by his **dream** — he **believes** that **anything** he does in **pursuit** of it is **entirely justified** — this includes a **life of crime** and **breaking apart a family**.

3) Only **Wilson explicitly mentions God**, but he **doesn't belong** to a church — he only **calls on God** when he **needs him**, and he sees God as a **vengeful presence**: **"God knows what you've been doing, everything you've been doing"**.

4) Tom even **uses religion** to help **pursue** his **adulterous relationship** with Myrtle — he **lies** that Daisy's **"a Catholic"** to **justify** the fact that he **won't leave her**.

Religion has been Replaced by Consumerism and the Pursuit of Pleasure

1) The characters **live aimless lives** that **revolve around pleasing themselves** and **acquiring new possessions**. For example, the guests at Gatsby's **parties** focus on **drinking**, looking for **new lovers**, and trying to make **"easy money"**.

2) The conversation between **Michaelis** and **Wilson** in **Chapter 8** suggests that **consumerism** has **replaced religion**:

> **"'You may fool me, but you can't fool God!'... Michaelis saw with a shock that he was looking at the eyes of Doctor T.J. Eckleburg..."**

Wilson **mistakes the eyes** of the **advertisement** for **God**. This shows that the eyes actually have **no meaning** except for the meaning that the characters **give** them. This could **reflect** the **feeling** of the 'lost generation' that **life is essentially meaningless** and is defined only by the **values** that people **give it**.

3) **Consumerism** promises that **material objects** will make you **happy** and give your life **meaning**. However, **material possessions** don't make people **happy** — in the novel this is **symbolised** by the fact that **cars**, a desirable **consumer item**, cause **death** and **destruction**.

4) The idea that **consumerism** has replaced **religious values** is **reinforced** throughout *The Great Gatsby*:

The eyes look out over the valley of ashes — this could represent God looking at the moral decay of the world.

© Suki Maltby-Duggan

   - Fitzgerald mentions the **"presbyterian nymphs"** in the **speakeasy** (a place where people could **illegally buy** and **drink alcohol** during **prohibition**) in **Chapter 4**. This use of **religious language** could suggest that **religious symbols** have **lost their power**, and are at home in places of **corruption**.

   - **Weddings** are a **religious** and legal union of a couple, but **Daisy's** wedding to **Tom** is used primarily to **display** their **extravagant wealth**. Tom brings **"four private cars"** and hires **"a whole floor"** of a hotel.

   - Gatsby's **car "scattered light"** across the landscape and has **"fenders spread like wings"**. These descriptions give the car **qualities** often associated with **religion** — it's a **source** of **light** and is winged like an **angel**.

Religion and Morality

Gatsby could be seen as a Religious Figure

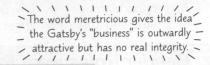

The word meretricious gives the idea the Gatsby's "business" is outwardly attractive but has no real integrity.

1) **Nick** links **Gatsby** directly to **God** when he says:

> "He was a son of God — a phrase which, if it means anything, means just that — and he must be about his **Father's business**, the service of a vast, vulgar, and meretricious beauty"

This **statement** could be **ironic** — the "**Father**" that Nick is referring to could be **Dan Cody** or **Wolfshiem**, **immoral self-made businessmen** who were **father figures** to Gatsby. Gatsby's "**business**" is the **pursuit** of **wealth**.

2) Alternatively, Fitzgerald could have **intended** to **connect Gatsby** with **Jesus** or **Adam**:

Gatsby and Jesus

- There are **biblical allusions** that develop the **similarities** between the two — Jesus became **mortal** and **sacrificed** himself for **mankind's sins**, whereas Gatsby tied himself to Daisy's **mortal**, "**perishable breath**", and **died** because he took the **blame** for **Daisy's sins**.
- Fitzgerald admired the **philosopher Ernest Renan**, who wrote a book called *The Life of Jesus* (1863). In this book, Renan **argued** that **Jesus** was just an **ordinary man** who **believed** he was the **son of God**. Renan wrote that Jesus was "**faithful to his self-created dream but scornful of the factual truth that finally crushes him and his dream**" — an **idea** that can be easily **applied** to **Gatsby**.

Gatsby and Adam

- The American Dream of **creating** a **land of opportunity**, a **perfect world** where anything is **possible**, echoes the **nature** of the **Garden of Eden**.
- A **woman** is responsible for the **downfall** of both **Adam** and **Gatsby** — **Eve** and **Daisy** respectively.

3) Fitzgerald could have **meant** the **term** "**son of God**" less **literally** — in **Christianity**, everyone is a "**son of God**" in the sense that Christians believe man is made in **God's image**. If Gatsby is just an **ordinary man**, this suggests that his "**gift for hope**" is even more "**extraordinary**".

4) In the novel's **shallow**, **materialistic** and **immoral society**, **religion** has been replaced by **consumerism**, so Gatsby's **wealth** and **dreams** could make him a **corrupted Christ-like figure** within a **corrupted** world. However, any **allusions** to **Gatsby** as a **religious figure** are the result of **Nick's narration**, and may just reflect Nick's own **moral confusion**.

The Seven Deadly Sins crop up Throughout the Novel

1) At **different points** in the **novel**, the characters indulge in all of the **seven deadly sins**. For example Myrtle is **envious** when she **sees Jordan** outside Wilson's **garage** — her eyes are "**wide with jealous terror**", and Tom is **proud** of his **mansion**: "**I've got a nice place here**".

2) In the **Bible** the **seven deadly sins** often **caused** the **downfall** of a **society**, for example, the city of **Sodom**. This **hints** that Fitzgerald believed the **decadence** of the '**Jazz Age**' couldn't **last**.

3) Nick **mentions** the "**cardinal virtues**" when he says "**I am one of the few honest people that I have ever known**". This is **ironic**, because honesty isn't a cardinal virtue, and because Nick is just as **dishonest** as the other characters.

Practice Questions

Q1 Fitzgerald once wrote "the redeeming things are not 'happiness and pleasure' but the deeper satisfactions that come out of struggle." To what extent does *The Great Gatsby* back up this insight?

Q2 Fitzgerald liked the cover art of *The Great Gatsby* so much that he told his publisher he had "written it into" the novel. How would the meaning of the novel have changed if Fitzgerald hadn't placed so much emphasis on Dr. T.J. Eckleburg?

"You may fool me, but you can't fool God!"

Silly George, you don't see God endorsing many products these days... 'Order your burning bush now, supplies are running low!', 'Holy Water — a delicious way to ward off vampires!' and 'Old Investament Savings — make sure your neighbour covets your ox — today!'

Gender and Sexuality

*Fitzgerald's marriage may have been unhappy, but it certainly gave him lots of material for examining gender roles...
Make sure you know a bit about how society was changing in the 1920s and how the characters reflect this.*

Gender Roles were Redefined in the 1920s

1) *The Great Gatsby* was written at a time of **social change**, when **traditional** gender roles were being **challenged**:

- During the **First World War**, **women** took on all kinds of **jobs** to **replace** the men who had gone to fight. This meant that it became **acceptable** for women to do a **wider range** of jobs, even after the war ended.
- In 1920, women in **all states** of America were granted the **right** to **vote**.
- The **flappers** challenged ideas of what was **feminine** — they cut their hair **short**, dressed to exaggerate **boyish** figures, were often **sexually active**, and realised they could have **independent** lives instead of getting **married**.

2) In the novel, some women are **portrayed** as **liberated** — the **female guests** at Gatsby's parties are described as "**wanderers, confident girls**"— they **aren't tied** to **men**. However, **despite** their **liberated appearance**, there are hints that **sexist values** exist — wives are "**lifted kicking into the night**" by their husbands.

The **Female Characters** highlight **Tensions** caused by the new **Gender Roles**

Fitzgerald uses Jordan, Daisy and Myrtle to explore the **conflict** between the existing **male-dominated society** and women's **hopes** for an **independent** lifestyle:

DAISY
- Young Daisy had a "**little white roadster**" and she was **sexually liberated**, **freely flirting** with army officers.
- Daisy **controls men** with her **looks** and **charm** — she **captivates** Nick, Tom and Gatsby. However, both Tom and Gatsby seem to **see her** as a **possession** rather than as an **individual**.
- Her **life** is **defined entirely** by her **relationships** with men — when she was **young** she "**wanted her life shaped**", and saw **marriage** as the **only way** she could do this. Nick says he has "**dinner with the Tom Buchanans**" — this suggests that **Daisy's identity** is now as **Tom's wife**, not as a **person** in her **own right**.

JORDAN
- Jordan has a **successful** golf **career**, and is therefore **quite independent**. **Descriptions** of her focus on **masculine characteristics**, "**an erect carriage... like a young cadet**", and even her name isn't **gender specific**. This suggests that she has the **male attributes required** to **remain independent**.
- It's hinted that Jordan is **sexually active** when Nick says she satisfies the "**demands of her hard, jaunty body**", but Nick also suggests that she has to **lie** to **hide** her **behaviour**: "**she had begun dealing in subterfuges... in order to keep that cool, insolent smile turned to the world**".

MYRTLE
- Myrtle seems to have **power** over her husband in their **marriage** — Wilson is "**his wife's man and not his own**", and yet he's still **able** to **lock her up** in **Chapter 7**.
- Myrtle's **affair** with Tom also suggests that she's **sexually liberated**. However, the **only way** she can **improve** her **situation** is through her **relationships with men** — she **relies** on **Tom** to **buy her things** and to **take her away** from the valley of ashes.

*'The Great Gatsby' is **Set** in a **Male-Dominated Society***

1) The novel's **focus** is mostly **male** — Gatsby is the **protagonist**, Nick is the **narrator**, and Tom helps to **drive** the **plot forward** — both by his **affair** with Myrtle, and by **forcing** a **confrontation** with Gatsby.

2) The **women** are **props** used to **reveal** the **male** characters' **personalities** e.g. Daisy's main role is as the **object** of Gatsby's **desire**.

3) Even the **geography** in *The Great Gatsby* is **dominated** by **men** — Nick imagines the **first settlers** arriving on the "**fresh, green breast**" of America, and the invading 'male' taking over and **colonising** the naked 'female' **country**.

4) However, because the story is told through a **male narrator**, the novel could present a **distorted view** of **women** — Fitzgerald himself **admitted** that it was "**a man's book**" and it contained "**no important woman character**".

Gender and Sexuality

Sexuality is connected to Power and Control

1) The **women** in the novel use their **sexuality** to get **what** they **want** — Myrtle wants to be **spoilt**, so she uses her **vitality** to make Tom **buy her things**. Daisy wants **attention**, so she murmurs "**to make people lean toward her**":

- Myrtle's **sexuality** is described as a **power** or a **force**, rather than a physical **attractiveness**. Nick says she is full of "**vitality... as if the nerves of her body were continually smouldering**".
- Daisy's **voice** represents her **feminine sexuality** — it gives her **power** over men. Nick describes it as "**a singing compulsion, a whispered 'Listen', a promise that she had done gay, exciting things**".

2) Myrtle is **sexualised** even **in death**: "**her left breast was swinging loose**". This **suggests** that her **sexuality destroyed her**.

3) The **sexuality** of the **men** in the novel seems to be **linked** with their **desire** and **ability to control** women:

- Tom's **sexuality** is **linked** to his **physicality**: "**Not even the effeminate swank of his riding clothes could hide the enormous power of that body — he seemed to fill those glistening boots until he strained the top lacing.**" This shows that he's **physically strong**, but words like "glistening" and "strained" have **sexual connotations**.
- Tom's **affairs** are about **control** as much as sex. He **bosses** Myrtle about, and **controls** her through **violence**. When he **realises** that both Daisy and Myrtle are "**slipping... from his control**" he feels "**hot whips of panic**". His panic **manifests** itself as **anger** at Gatsby — he assumes Gatsby is **responsible** for **taking his wife**, and **doesn't consider** that **Daisy** is **capable** of making her **own decisions**.
- Gatsby's **desire** for Daisy is linked to a desire to **control** her: "**He took what he could get, ravenously and unscrupulously — eventually he took Daisy... took her because he had no real right to touch her hand.**" By **repeatedly emphasising** that Gatsby "**took her**", Fitzgerald places Gatsby in **control**. He's **active, powerful** and **initiates** the sexual relationship — Daisy has **no control**, she's the **passive object** that was taken.

There are Hints of Homosexuality throughout the novel

1) Critics such as **Keath Fraser** have **interpreted** parts of the text as an **indication** that Nick's **sexuality** is **ambiguous**:

- Nick says that he's often privy to "**the intimate revelations of young men... marred by obvious suppressions**".
- He's **attracted** to Jordan's **boyish** figure — he thinks her body is "**hard**" and notes the "**slender muscles in her arms**".
- There's a vague, confused scene with Mr McKee — a "**feminine man**" — where Nick finds himself "**standing beside his bed**" while Mr McKee is "**between the sheets, clad in his underwear**".

2) On the other hand, Nick mentions several **relationships** with **girls**, and thinks he might be "**in love**" with **Jordan**.

3) Other critics have argued that Jordan's **sexuality** is also **ambiguous** — she's described in **masculine terms** and seems to **form closer relationships** with **women** than with **men**.

4) The **sexual ambiguity** throughout the novel seems to **reflect** a **society** where **social** and **sexual barriers** are **breaking down**.

© PARAMOUNT / THE KOBAL COLLECTION

Practice Questions

Q1 How does Fitzgerald portray the female characters as challenging or conforming to 1920s society's views of women?

Q2 How does Fitzgerald portray ambiguities in Nick's sexuality?

Q3 How do Gatsby and Tom each challenge the gender expectations of their society? How do they conform to them?

"Dishonesty in a woman is a thing you never blame deeply"

I batted my eyelashes and tried this line when I was caught cheating at an important golf tournament, but they wouldn't have any of it. I was banished from the mini-golf course, stripped of my mini-title and my mini-trophy. I do miss misogyny, it had its uses...

Structure and Narration in 'The Great Gatsby'

Fitzgerald's been a bit clever with the novel's structure — he's not just told the story from beginning to end, with some action in the middle — that'd be too easy... Oh no, he's used a fancy complex structure.

Fitzgerald uses a **Narrator** to tell the story **Retrospectively**

1) Fitzgerald's novel may be about **Gatsby**, but Fitzgerald doesn't write his story in Gatsby's own **voice**. Instead, he uses a **narrator**, Nick Carraway.

2) **Nick's voice** is **not the same** as the **author's voice**:

> Instead of writing as an **omniscient narrator**, Fitzgerald uses a **narrator** who **doesn't know** all the facts. In this way, he **sketches** Gatsby as a **shadowy figure** that the reader can only **glimpse** through Nick's **memories**.

3) **Nick's viewpoint** is **not the same** as **Gatsby's perspective**. Nick has **survived** Gatsby and is able to tell the story of his life — and **death** — **after** it has all **ended**. Nick has a **retrospective viewpoint**.

4) Gatsby's **death** happens **before** the **beginning** of the novel. This gives Gatsby's death a **predetermined quality** — it is **inescapable**. This structure makes Gatsby seem like a **tragic hero** (see p.49).

© PARAMOUNT / THE KOBAL COLLECTION

Nick **Introduces Gatsby** to the reader **Bit by Bit**

1) Nick **combines three** different **strands** of **storytelling** in his **retrospective narrative**, **disrupting** the plot's **chronology**:

- Most of the novel is made up of Nick's own **experiences** of life in the **East**. This strand is organised in **chronological order** according to **Nick's perspective**.
- **Gatsby's backstory** is told through **different perspectives**, e.g. the **party guests' speculations** about Gatsby's **secret identity** and **Jordan's description** of Gatsby's **affair** with **Daisy**. Nick adds in some accounts, like Gatsby's description of his own **adolescent ambitions**, **out** of the **order** in which they're revealed to him.
- Nick **reflects** on the story, **returns** to **read** his work, makes **revisions** and adds **lists** made **at the time** of the events. This **emphasises** the fact that Nick's telling his story from a **retrospective viewpoint**.

2) Nick has all of this **knowledge** at the time of writing, but he chooses to **order** the **narrative** so that the reader only learns about Gatsby's life **before** West Egg **bit by bit**.

3) This makes Gatsby seem **more mysterious** as Nick **hides** parts of Gatsby's **identity** until he chooses to let the reader know. Gatsby may be the "**man who gives his name to this book**", but Nick is the one who **controls** it.

4) The initial **mystery** of Gatsby's identity **piques** the reader's **interest**, but Nick weaves Gatsby's **backstory** into the **narrative** of his **later life**. This makes the character seem more **rounded** and **real**.

The novel **Turns** around the **Central Chapter**

1) The book is split into **nine chapters**, and the **structure** is **arranged** around Gatsby and Daisy's **reunion** in Chapter 5. The **first half** of the novel builds up to their **eventual meeting**, and the **second half** of the novel deals with the **consequences** of their reunion.

2) **Chapters 1 to 4** are written almost entirely from **Nick's viewpoint**. At the **end** of **Chapter 4**, **Jordan's narrative** of Daisy and Gatsby's **previous relationship** begins a **shift** in the novel towards **multiple narratives**. This **gradual shift** in narrative helps to **reveal Gatsby's past** and his **current** character.

3) **Chapter 5** is written entirely in the **past tense** without interruption by the other **strands** of Nick's **narrative**. The return to a **first-person perspective** (following Jordan's narrative), and the **focus** on a **few moments** of time **intensifies** the **emotion** of Gatsby and Daisy's reunion.

4) **Chapters 6** to **9 break down** the **myth** of Gatsby's **glamorous** and **mysterious lifestyle**:

> Nick provides **alternative viewpoints** in Chapters 6 to 9, including **Michaelis's account** of the **inquest** into Myrtle's death, and Gatsby's **recollection** of his **early affair** with Daisy. In this way, **Fitzgerald** is able to provide **different perspectives** on the **same events**. This builds up a more **rounded** picture and helps the **reader** to **fill** in the gaps in Nick's **personal account**.

Structure and Narration in 'The Great Gatsby'

Nick seems like a *Trustworthy Narrator...*

1) Nick **claims** that he's **tolerant**, **open-minded** and a **good listener**. This suggests that he's **well suited** to **narrating**.

2) Nick is **well educated** and **articulate**. He's comfortable using **colloquial language** as part of a **diverse vocabulary**:

> • **Colloquial language**, like dialect and slang, makes the character's **speech** sound more **natural** and **informal**.
>
> • Nick's **diverse vocabulary** gives the **novel a fluent, poetic tone**.

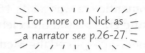
For more on Nick as a narrator see p.26-27.

3) Nick seems like an ideal **narrator** because he's at a distance from the people he's talking about. He's **connected** to **wealthy people**, like Daisy, but isn't **rich enough** to live amongst them. He's **friends** with people like **Gatsby**, but is **too conservative** to really take part in their **wild lifestyle**. He's on the **edge** of **both social circles**, which gives him an ideal **perspective** — not quite **outside** or **inside**.

...but he *Doesn't See Everything* that happens

1) Even though Nick's the **narrator**, he's still a **character** in the novel and he's **only aware** of events he **witnesses first hand**. Fitzgerald **limits** his **narrator's view** to encourage the **reader** to make their **own judgements**.

2) Nick is not as **distanced** from the **action** as he appears to be. The other characters are still his **friends, family** and **members** of the **society** he lives in. This means that his **take** on events is **subjective** rather than **objective**:

> • Nick finishes **narrating** the novel **two years after** the **events** of the summer of 1922 — he is relying on his **memory**. He could have **forgotten** important details.
>
> • He is a **self-conscious storyteller**. Nick makes **revisions** to his **writing** which reminds his readers that he is **selecting** the **information** and **determining** the way he **structures** the story of Gatsby's life. Nick uses dialogue to **break up** the **narrative** and give a **clearer idea** of the **other characters' personalities**, but he also **quotes** long speeches *verbatim* (word for word) which the reader cannot rely on for **accuracy**.
>
> • He uses **other people's accounts** of events without **questioning** them. He doesn't realise that **newspaper reports** and **inquest statements** might be **biased**. He includes **Jordan's** description of Gatsby and Daisy's early relationship, despite the fact that he believes Jordan is "**incurably dishonest**".
>
> • Nick's novel might be just a **record** of the **rumours** that surrounded Gatsby's life. There's **no proof** that his **account** is **reliable** — it could be an **exaggeration** of the **truth** that will add to the **rumours** around Gatsby.

Nick *Changes* in the *Course* of the *Novel*

1) Nick becomes **more judgemental** and **less tolerant** as the **novel progresses** — by the end he has **no patience** left and says of Tom "**I couldn't forgive him or like him**".

2) **By the end of the novel, Nick is** much more **outspoken** with his **criticism** than his **compliments**. He may be **tolerant** of people in **public**, but on **paper** he delivers a **harsh critique** with a **contemptuous tone**.

3) Nick seems to **believe** that he can **maintain** his **traditional Midwest values** in the East, and **holds himself** in **high regard**. By holding the **moral high ground**, Nick slips easily into **intolerance** and **judgement** of other people.

Practice Questions

Q1 Nick is the reader's guide to Gatsby's life. How do you think the story would change if the narrator had been Gatsby?

Q2 The reader learns about Myrtle's death through details taken from newspaper reports and inquest testimonials. How would the reader's reaction to Myrtle's death be different if Nick had witnessed it first hand?

Q3 What effect does the structure of the novel have on the reader's understanding of Gatsby as a character?

"that familiar conviction that life was beginning over again with the summer"

So, Gatsby's the main man, but Nick's the narrator. Jordan talks a bit, but Nick writes what she says in his words because he's remembering it all. But ultimately, they're all just characters — Fitzgerald's pulling the strings, like some hidden puppet master.

Genre and Literary Influences

There was a lot going on in the 1920s, what with the aftermath of the war, the boom years, the androgynous fashions...
The same can be said for the literature of the time, and 'The Great Gatsby' is a classic example of this.

Fitzgerald was *Inspired* by the *Romantic Poets*

1) The **Romantic** era was a late 18th- to early 19th-century **artistic movement**. The **poets** of the **Romantic era** focused on **celebrating** the **beauty** of **nature** and favoured **emotion** over **reason**.

2) Romanticism explored the **Medieval literary tradition** of the quest for the **grail** and a knight's **fidelity**. These ideas are referred to in *The Great Gatsby* — Gatsby "**committed himself to the following of a grail**" in his pursuit of Daisy.

3) Fitzgerald was influenced by the Romantic poet, **John Keats**.

> **John Keats, 'Ode to a Nightingale'**
>
> In Keats's poem the **nightingale's song** transports the speaker into a deep daydream about the nature of **death** and the **uncertainty** of **life**. He's **torn** between **extreme emotions** — he's "**too happy**", but his "**heart aches**".

4) Fitzgerald alludes to **Keats's nightingale** in *The Great Gatsby*.

> • Daisy sees a **nightingale** and says "**It's romantic, isn't it, Tom?**", as if she's referring to its **poetic significance**.
>
> • The moment ends when the "**shrill**" **telephone** rings. Modern technology **undermines** the **Romantic** reference. Fitzgerald borrows **Romantic poetic imagery**, but **juxtaposes** it with **20th-century** technology.

Fitzgerald was *Writing* during the *Modernist Period*

1) The **early 20th century** saw **rapid technological change**, driven by the demands of the **war**. Some **writers** responded to **this** by **experimenting** with **unconventional** language and structure. The **era** was called **Modernism**.

2) Fitzgerald was **excited** by the new **Modernist writing style** — but he still wanted to make "**something new**". He merged **poetic Romanticism** with the **sparse** style of the **Modernists** and incorporated **advertising slogans** and **slang**:

> • Chapter 2 opens with the **lyrical description** of the "**ash-grey men**" who work with "**transcendent effort**". This follows the **Romantic tradition** of **idealised images** of **workmen**. However, Fitzgerald's workmen are **not farm labourers** working the **fields** — rather than being **close to nature**, they are covered in **urban grime**.
>
> • Fitzgerald uses **slang** to describe **T.J. Eckleburg** as a "**wild wag of an oculist**" whose **advertising** looms over the valley. In a **postwar world**, the **existence of God** was in **question**. Fitzgerald uses **Eckleburg's image** as a '**substitute**' god. To make this link **explicit**, even the **substitute** god has **abandoned** his people because Eckleburg "**sank down himself into eternal blindness, or forgot them and moved away**".

3) Fitzgerald admired the **modernist** poet T.S. Eliot — he called himself a "**worshipper**" of **Eliot's poetry**.

> **T.S. Eliot**
>
> Eliot's long poem, '**The Waste Land**' was published in 1922. The poem's representation of a **sterile landscape**, where everyone is **isolated** and **unable to love**, voiced a **common concern** of the 1920s.

4) Eliot's '**waste land**' may have inspired Fitzgerald's idea of the **desolate valley of ashes** in *The Great Gatsby*:

T.S. Eliot

> **'The Waste Land'**
>
> • Eliot's poem considers the **uncertain future**:
>
> > 'What shall we do to-morrow? What shall we ever do?'
> > T.S. Eliot, 'The Waste Land'
>
> • The **people** of Eliot's 'waste land' "**know only / A heap of broken images**".

> **The Great Gatsby**
>
> • When Daisy **considers** the **future** in Chapter 7, her words **echo** Eliot's lines:
>
> > 'What'll we do with ourselves this afternoon?' cried Daisy, 'and the day after that, and the next thirty years?'
> > F. Scott Fitzgerald, *The Great Gatsby*
>
> • Fitzgerald suggests that the **powerful images** of **communications** and **advertising** have replaced the '**real**' **person** or **idea**, e.g. Jordan looks like a "**good illustration**" and God is an **advert**.

5) The **valley of ashes** is central to Fitzgerald's vision of a **desolate** world, full of images but **empty** of **meaning**.

© Mary Evans Picture Library

Genre and Literary Influences

Some people see 'The Great Gatsby' as a 20th-Century Tragedy

1) Classical tragedies follow the **fall** of a **noble man** who is **punished** by the **gods** for making a **mistake**. His life was commented on by a **Chorus**, a group of actors who talked **directly** to the **audience**.

2) However, by the **20th century**, writers had started to see 'tragedy' differently:

> **20th-Century Tragedy**
> - The early **twentieth century** was full of **tragic events** that **affected everyone**. People began to see that the term 'tragedy' could be used to describe an **individual's suffering** irrespective of their **status** or **gender**.
> - A **modern tragic hero** could also be a **victim** — their downfall wasn't always the result of a **personal mistake** but could be due to a **conflict** between the **individual** and the **society** they lived in.
> - In **classical tragedy**, **man** is in **conflict** with the **gods**, but in **modern tragedy**, the hero's **downfall** comes about because of a **range** of **other factors**.
> - The role of the '**Chorus**' could be filled by **another character** in the play, or **shared** between **characters**.

3) In this sense, *The Great Gatsby* is a modern 'tragedy'. Gatsby is a **victim** as well as a **hero** of the '**Jazz Age**' because he is as **flawed** as the **society** he **lives** in.

4) In a **modernisation** of **classical tragedy**, *The Great Gatsby* replaces religion with consumerism, so **adverts** seem to take on an almost **divine power** (see p.42).

5) Fitzgerald makes use of the '**choric voice**' to help **narrate** Gatsby's life:

> **Choric Voice**
> - In **classical tragedy**, the '**Chorus**' was a group who **narrated** the events and **commented** on them.
> - In some ways, **Nick's** role as **narrator** makes him '**chorus-like**' — he stands to the **side** of the **main events** and **comments** on what he **sees**.
> - In another way, the '**choric voice**' is **composed** of the **mixture** of **different characters' voices** in the novel — for example, Gatsby's party guests, Wolfshiem and Jordan all add their **voices** to the crowd that speculates on Gatsby's past

It's also a Novel about Writing a Novel

1) Nick is a **self-conscious storyteller**. He claims to have been "**rather literary in college**", shows off his **writing** using **unusual words** and a **poetic style** and refers to "**this book**" that he's writing.

2) As the **actual author**, **Fitzgerald** has **written** a **novel** that refers to the act of **writing** a **novel**.

> **Metafiction**
> **Metafiction** is a type of prose that refers to **itself** and its **author** in the process of telling its story. Metafiction might also be referred to as a '**self-reflexive**' style — it **draws attention** to itself as an **object** and a **work** of **fiction**.

Fitzgerald may have been influenced by Joseph Conrad's Heart of Darkness. Like Nick, Marlow is a self-conscious and unreliable narrator.

3) *The Great Gatsby*'s **self-reflexive** style means that the **novel** can **directly address itself** as a **work of art**. This causes the reader to **question** the **relationship** between **fiction** and **fact**.

Practice Questions

Q1 How does reading 'The Waste Land' affect the way you read *The Great Gatsby*?

Q2 Was Gatsby's tragic downfall due more to his faults or the failings of his society?

Q3 '*The Great Gatsby* is a book about writing a book'. What effect does this have on your reading of it?

"His right hand suddenly ordered divine retribution to stand by."

The thing about tragedy is, well, someone's got to die. And usually you know when it's coming. When they've made their mistakes and realised they've done something wrong, then they just have to wait it out for death to come and find them. Them's the rules.

Fitzgerald's Use of Language

Fitzgerald adds a right hodge-podge of foreign words, slang and technical terms into his dreamlike prose. This mixture gives the reader a good sense of the incessant society chatter that surrounds the quiet loneliness of Gatsby's life.

Fitzgerald's **Writing Style** *is sometimes more like* **Poetry** *than* **Prose**

1) *The Great Gatsby* is written in **prose**. However, Fitzgerald was **inspired** by **poetic techniques**. He borrows the **style** and **rhythm** of **poetry** to create a '**poetic prose**'.

2) Fitzgerald chooses his words **carefully** as a **poet** might do, to create **vivid** and **arresting images**:

> The **range** of words in the novel, from "**punctilious**" to "**bantering**", creates **unusual rhythms** and **sounds**, making the **language** sound **new**. **Foreign vocabulary** helps to create a **cosmopolitan atmosphere** and makes Nick's **vocabulary** seem **rich** and **broad** — Fitzgerald uses **French** words, e.g. "**coupé**" for car, "**hauteur**" for arrogance and "**amour**" for love.

3) Fitzgerald also uses unusual **words** — in the final paragraph of the novel, he describes the future as "**orgastic**", an **adjective** that **echoes** two more familiar words — '**orgiastic**' and '**orgasm**'. This encapsulates the idea of **wild** and **uncontrolled** activity and **sexual climax**.

4) Fitzgerald is able to use a '**poetic prose**' style without it seeming **odd** because his **narrator**, Nick, is an educated **character** who claims to be "**rather literary**".

Fitzgerald uses **Repetition** *to give his* **Prose** *a* **Poetic Rhythm**

1) **Alliteration** and **anaphora** are both types of **poetic repetition** that Fitzgerald uses to give his **writing rhythm.** **Alliteration** is the **repetition** of **sounds** and **anaphora** is the **repetition** of **words**:

Anaphora		Alliteration
Repeating the **same word** at the beginning of **linked clauses** creates a powerful **pulsing** effect.	Even when the East excited me most, even when I was most keenly aware of its superiority to the bored, sprawling, swollen towns beyond the Ohio, with their interminable inquisitions which spared only the child and the very old — even then it had always for me a quality of distortion.	**Repeating** the **same sound** at the beginning of **adjacent words** binds the words together and makes the **language** sound **purposely poetic**.

2) Fitzgerald uses **repetition** to **emphasise images** and **ideas**. Nick describes the motion of the air-bed which held Gatsby's body, as on an "**accidental course with its accidental burden**". The **repetition** contradicts the idea that Gatsby's **tragic death** was **predestined**, and suggests that it was the **result** of a **series** of **careless actions** by **careless people**.

Fitzgerald uses **Unusual Combinations** *of* **Words**

Words convey **images**, **sounds**, **emotion** or **abstract ideas**. By putting **new combinations** of **words** together, Fitzgerald pushes his **reader** to **connect** separate **ideas** in **new** and **interesting ways**:

Oxymorons

- An **oxymoron** is where **two words** that **contradict** each other are used together. Fitzgerald uses **oxymorons** to give **complex descriptions** of things in a **concise way**, but leave them open to **interpretation**.

- For example, Nick describes Myrtle as having a "**soft, coarse voice**". The use of this oxymoron makes Myrtle's **voice** match her **two contradictory lives** as the "**coarse**" **wife** of a **mechanic** and the "**soft**" **mistress** of an **upper-class** man.

Synaesthesia

- **Synaesthesia** is a literary technique that **mixes up** the **senses** to make **familiar** things seem strange and new. This **technique** borrows its name from a medical condition which causes people to **experience** some **stimuli** with a **different sense** e.g. to be able to '**taste**' sounds or '**hear**' colours.

- Fitzgerald's **synaesthetic** language mixes **different senses**. Phrases like "**yellow cocktail music**", "**warm darkness**" and "**pale gold odour**" mix together **sight**, **sound**, **smell** and **taste** to create a **whirl** of different **senses**. This brings the scene **vividly** to **life** for the reader.

Fitzgerald's Use of Language

Fitzgerald uses *Colour* and *Music* to *Set the Scene*

1) **Colour** is a central part of Fitzgerald's writing **technique** — it adds to the **vibrancy** of the **images** he is describing.

Ambiguous Colours

'Harlequin' is a **bright shade** of **green** and can also mean **patterned with diamonds**. This **ambiguity** suggests the **bright colour** and **geometric pattern** of the salads.

On buffet tables, garnished with glistening hors-d'oeuvre, spiced baked hams crowded against salads of harlequin designs and pastry pigs and turkeys bewitched to a dark gold.

Rich Colours

Colours like "**dark gold**" add **rich**, **deep tones**. The references to "**gold**" and the diamond pattern of the "**harlequin designs**" make these colours seem '**rich**' in **another sense** — the food is described as if it is made of **money**.

2) Fitzgerald uses **colours** as a **code** throughout the **novel**, e.g. **green** stands for both **Gatsby's dream** as symbolised by the **green light** at the end of Daisy's dock, and the **American Dream** as seen in the "**green breast of the new world**" — the **shared colour** links the **two 'dreams'** (see p.52).

3) Music plays an **important** role in **defining** the **mood** of the novel. Fitzgerald uses **music** and **song lyrics** to create **atmosphere** and remind the reader of the historical and political **context** (see p.15).

Lyrical Voices

The **party guests'** chatter is described as an "**opera of voices**" and Daisy's voice is referred to as "**a deathless song**", as if the **rhythm** and **melody** of **music** accompany the way the characters **speak**. Nick's **poetic prose** makes **everything** seem more **romantic** and **lyrical**, and the fact that people's **voices** sound like **song** helps **preserve** the **idea** that his story is like a **romantic opera** or a **ballet**.

The use of *Language* emphasises the characters' *Connection* with the *Past*

1) The characters seem to be **striving** to recapture the **past**. Fitzgerald uses words like "**forever**" and "**always**" **regularly**.

2) Nick says that Tom's life "**savours of anticlimax**", forcing him to "**drift on forever seeking**" to recover his **youth**.

3) By choosing to write most of the novel in the **past tense** rather than as if the events are **currently happening**, Nick keeps the other characters **locked** in the **past**, but **allows himself** to talk about his **own present**: "**Reading over what I have written so far**".

The only point at which Nick uses the present tense for the other characters is in Chapter 3 to give the impression of a never ending party at Gatsby's house: "now the orchestra is playing".

4) Daisy asks "**Do you always watch for the longest day of the year and then miss it?**" She answers her own question by **repeating** the question's **phrasing**. This **repetition** (see p.50) suggests that she "**always**" repeats this **mistake**, just as she **repeats mistakes** in other areas of her **life**.

5) The novel **ends** with the line, "**So we beat on, boats against the current, borne back ceaselessly into the past.**" Fitzgerald expands **Gatsby's personal tragedy** to cover the struggle of every individual **fighting** against the **current** that will turn the present into '**history**'. For more analysis of this final line see p.23.

© PARAMOUNT / THE KOBAL COLLECTION

Practice Questions

Q1 Read the first six paragraphs of Chapter 3. Discuss the effect of Fitzgerald's poetic prose in this passage.

Q2 Choose a passage in the novel that appeals to the reader's senses and explain how Fitzgerald has achieved this.

Q3 How does Fitzgerald's language emphasise the passage of time in *The Great Gatsby*?

"I'd got a strong impression that he was picking his words with care"

Fitzgerald is considered one of the most innovative writers of his generation. Even today readers find his dreamy prose as fresh as it was in 1926. Never mind language analysis, we should be more worried about what sort of preservatives he was putting in this stuff.

Symbols and Imagery

Pretty sure if I wrote a book about a man who drives a banana car and lives on a giant egg, whiling away the days collecting fabulous shirts, I wouldn't be hailed a genius. Must be something to do with Fitzgerald's fine use of imagery...

Fitzgerald uses **Symbols** and **Imagery** to **Emphasise** the novel's **Themes**

1) Fitzgerald's writing is full of **references** to **bright colours**, **sensual music** and **fragrant scents**. He is involving the reader's **senses** to help make a scene seem more **tangible**.

> **Imagery**
>
> If a writer **describes** a **scene** or an **object** in such a way as to **appeal** to the reader's **senses**, he is using **imagery**. Imagery helps to set the **tone** and **mood** of a scene.

2) Fitzgerald also describes **objects** that hold **more significance** than others — he uses these objects as **symbols**:

> **Symbols**
>
> A **symbol** is an **object** or **image** that **represents** something **other than itself**. A symbol might provide some **information** or **relate** to an **idea**. E.g. cars symbolise both **status** and **death**.

The **Green Light** is a **Symbol** of **Hope**

1) At the beginning of *The Great Gatsby*, the **green light** is a **sign** for Daisy's presence:

Actual situation	Significance	Symbol
The **green light** is a **visible** object **near** where **Daisy lives**.	Gatsby **hasn't seen** Daisy in **years** and the **green light** is the **closest** he can get to her.	Gatsby doesn't think that Daisy is **like** a green light — but he lets the green light **represent** Daisy. The green light becomes a **symbol** for Daisy.

2) However, Daisy is already a **symbol**:

> Gatsby's idea of Daisy is **romanticised**. He has stopped seeing **Daisy** as a **real person**, and more as the **fantasy future**. Therefore, Daisy herself becomes a **symbol** of **Gatsby's hope** for the **future**.

If the **green light** stands for **Daisy**, and **Daisy** symbolises the **future**, then the **green light** is a **symbol** of the **future**.

3) When Gatsby is **reunited** with Daisy, the **distance** between **reality** and **fantasy** is made clear. Daisy's **not** the **single**, **young woman** of his **dreams** — she is **married**, with a **child**. At this point, the **symbol detaches** from what it **symbolised** — what Nick saw as one of Gatsby's "**enchanted objects**" becomes just a "**green light on a dock**".

4) The reader also makes more **traditional associations** with the colour green, e.g. **jealousy**, **inexperience**, **freshness** and **sickness**. These **associations** all **blend** together in the **symbolism** of Gatsby's **vision** of **Daisy**.

5) At the end of the novel, the colour green **resurfaces** in Nick's **vision** of the "**fresh, green breast of the new world**" — **America** as it must have seemed to the **sailors** who arrived centuries before. This **connects** Gatsby's **yearning** for Daisy and the symbolism of the colour green to the '**new world**' and the **pursuit** of the '**American Dream**'.

The **Colours** of **Precious Metals** increase in **Value** throughout the novel

1) Nick describes Daisy as a "**golden girl**", connecting her with the colour **gold**. She is a **radiant** character with a "**glowing**" **voice** and **face** , which draws on the fact that the name Daisy is from '**day's eye**'.

2) However, her "**golden**" image is also created by the fact that she's **associated** with **money**. Gatsby comments that Daisy's "**glowing**" voice is "**full of money**", which makes the **link** between the **colour gold** and **money explicit**.

3) Nick suggests that the young Gatsby saw Daisy as "**silver**", whereas over time, she becomes "**golden**". The **increasing value** of the **metallic metaphors** suggests that her **value** is connected to how **unattainable** she is.

> **Gold-Hatted Gatsby**
>
> At one point, Fitzgerald wanted to call his novel *Gold-Hatted Gatsby*. Instead, he decided to **open the** novel with an **epigraph** that starts "**Then wear the gold hat, if that will move her**". Putting a '**hat**' on is a way of saying '**to adopt a role**'. If Gatsby becomes the "**gold-hatted [...] lover**" of the epigraph, he must **adopt** the **role** of the **wealthy socialite** and **flaunt** his **material wealth** — which is **exactly** what he does.

Symbols and Imagery

Fitzgerald *Inverts* the *Symbolism* of the colour *White*

1) **White** is **traditionally** a **symbolic colour** associated with **purity** and **virginity**. However, the **meaning** of the **colour white changes** through the novel, eventually suggesting that white is used to **cover up** characters' **darker** traits.

- Nick's **first** arrival at the Buchanans' house is characterised by the **whiteness** of the surroundings. The ceiling is described as a **"frosted wedding-cake"** and Daisy and Jordan are **dressed** in white. Nick imagines that they've just taken a **"short flight around the house"** which makes them sound like **angels**.

- The room is later described as **"the crimson room"**. The **"wine-coloured rug"** dominates the **room**, which **anticipates** the **blood** on the **hands** of Daisy and **high society**, who are ultimately **responsible** for the **casual "holocaust"** of the **lower-class characters**, Gatsby, Myrtle and Wilson.

- By the end of the novel, Nick is so **disillusioned** that his associations with the **colour white** are **reversed** and the colour white starts to **represent** corruption. Nick dreams of a **drunken woman** lying **unconscious** on a stretcher in a **"white evening dress"**. Her **lack of awareness** and her dangling hand, **"cold with jewels"**, symbolise the **coldness** of the **upper classes** and the fact that **"no one cares"**.

2) The colour seems to be used as a '**whitewash**' to **hide** things that people don't want **society** to **see**:

- Both Jordan and Daisy uses cosmetic **"white powder"** to disguise their **flaws**. Jordan uses it to hide an **unfashionable tan** on her **fingers**, while Nick notices **"a tiny gust of powder"** rising from Daisy's **chest**.

- Myrtle wears a **"cream coloured"** dress when she's **pretending** to be **upper-class** in her **New York apartment** — she uses the **pale colour** to try to **hide** her **working-class background**.

- Nick's choice of **"white flannels"** at Gatsby's party could suggest that he's trying to **appear innocent**.

Everyone is *Scared* about *Looking* one another in the *Eye*

1) Eyes are traditionally thought of as '**windows to the soul**'. In *The Great Gatsby* the characters seem **scared** to make **eye contact** because of what **others** might **see** in them, or what they might **recognise** in **others**:

© PARAMOUNT / THE KOBAL COLLECTION

- Nick says at the first lunch at the Buchanan's house **"I was conscious of wanting to look squarely at everyone, and yet to avoid all eyes"**. Nick seems keen to **observe** the others but doesn't want to be **examined** too closely himself.

- Throughout the book, **Daisy's eyes** are described as **"bright"**. Yet, at the hotel, Gatsby asks her to say she never loved Tom and she **"looked at him blindly"**. Daisy is **worried** that her **eyes** will give her **secret** away.

- When the **phone rings during dinner**, Jordan and Nick exchange a look that is **"consciously devoid of meaning"** — they **don't want** to give anything away.

2) The **most sinister** eyes in the novel are **"the giant eyes of Doctor T.J. Eckleburg"**, that keep a **"vigil"** over the valley of ashes like an **omniscient observer** of **society**. Wilson sees the **old optician's advert** as the **eyes** of **God**, which could **symbolise** a society that needs its '**vision correcting**' in order to '**see**' its **faults**.

Practice Questions

Q1 How does the use of symbolism and imagery contribute to *The Great Gatsby*'s representation of the American Dream?

Q2 Do you think that Fitzgerald presents Doctor T.J. Eckleburg as a god or as proof of the absence of God in the novel?

Q3 Choose a character from *The Great Gatsby*. What symbols and images does Fitzgerald associate with that character and how does it help develop an idea of who they are?

"Her voice is full of money"

Daisy's voice is her asset. She reels them in with that sing-song voice of hers. It's full of money. Quite literally, apparently. She must look like a broken slot machine, just spewing out change. Oh, wait — what? Symbolism got me again. Fitzy, you tricksy writer, you.

Symbols and Imagery

Fitzgerald had a terrible drum kit. It was all cymbals. Badum-chhh. But seriously, there are a lot of symbols in this novel. Two pages just wasn't enough, so here's two more. And still, there are lots more to find.

Cars *are* Symbols *of* Status *and* Destruction

1) The **cars** in *The Great Gatsby* are **more** than just **transport** — they're also **symbolic commodities**.

Cars as Symbols of Status

- Tom uses his car to assert his **social** and **financial superiority** over Wilson. It allows him to get **access** to Myrtle, while Wilson's **lack** of **transport** means he can't take Myrtle **out** of Tom's **reach**. Tom **never intends** to **sell** the car to Wilson, but dangles it like **bait** to emphasise his **power** over the **lower classes**.

- Gatsby's **car** completes his **image** as a **successful, self-made man**. It is a **"rich cream colour, bright with nickel"** — the **combination** of **rich colours** links his car to **precious metals** (see p.52).

2) However, the **power** of the **cars** can be misused — e.g. Tom has a **car crash** that **injures** a **hotel maid** he was seeing just after his **wedding** and **Owl Eyes'** drunken **companion crashes** his car after Gatsby's **first party** in Chapter 3. These car crashes **reveal** the drivers' **antisocial vices** — **infidelity** and **drunkenness**.

3) Fitzgerald uses cars to symbolise a character's **ability** to **destroy** those around them, while keeping themselves **safe**.

Cars as Symbols of Destruction

- The **papers** nickname Gatsby's **car** the **"death car"**, making it **explicit** that the car can be a **fatal weapon**.

- The **language** used to describe Myrtle's **death reinforces** the **dangerous power** of the car and the **fragility** of **people**. Myrtle's breast is **"swinging loose like a flap"** and her mouth is **"ripped"**.

- Nick concludes that Tom and Daisy **"smashed up things and creatures and then retreated back into their money"**. Using **violent** but **simple language**, Nick refers to Daisy's **car crash** that so **easily kills** Myrtle, and **condemns** the **excess** of **wealth** that **protects** them, like the **heavy body** of an expensive **car**.

Fitzgerald *uses* Animal *and* Flower Imagery

1) Fitzgerald uses **natural imagery** in *The Great Gatsby* to **highlight** certain aspects of the **novel's characters**:

Animal Imagery

- Many of Gatsby's guests have **animal** names that **suggest** their **personality** (see p.35). The names **Whitebait** and **Hammerhead** could suggest that the **social circle** is full of **'small fry'** and **'big sharks'** in business.

- Animals themselves are **rare** in the novel. The Eggs are dominated by **bright displays** of **electrical lights** and **modern technology**. When Gatsby looks out towards Daisy's dock, Nick describes the **"loud, bright night, with wings beating in the trees"**. Fitzgerald's use of **aggressive adjectives** makes the birds seem **sinister**. Fitzgerald's use of **menacing animal imagery** suggests that **society itself** has grown **'unnatural'**.

2) **Floral imagery** is used throughout the novel, filling scenes with **scent** and **colour**. Fitzgerald links **sensual floral images** to **character's personalities**.

Plant Imagery

- Gatsby buys a **"greenhouse"** of flowers to **impress Daisy**. This suggests that Gatsby thinks he can **buy Daisy's affections**.

- Nick interprets Gatsby's **feelings** after having **kissed** Daisy for the first time, saying that Daisy **"blossomed for him like a flower"**.

- Daisy admires a **film star** who is a **"scarcely human orchid of a woman"**. This **highlights** how **exotic** she is and **hints** that she couldn't **survive outside** of her **privileged existence**.

- **Daisy** begins to **embody** the **flower** she is **named** after (see p.28). The daisy is **delicate** and **coloured white**, but it's also associated with **death** because of the common phrase **'pushing up daisies'**. Daisy is both the **source** and **death** of Gatsby's **dream**.

© Everett Collection / Rex Features

Symbols and Imagery

The **Long Island Necks** are turned into **'Eggs'**

1) Fitzgerald's decision to change **Great** and **Manhasset Neck** (p.2) into **"a pair of enormous eggs"** is **symbolic**:

- Eggs are symbols of **birth** or **'rebirth'**. At the **start** of the novel Nick says that his **life** is **"beginning over again"** when he moves to West Egg — he imagines himself as a **colonial "settler"** arriving in America.
- Nick refers to the **birds** that fly overhead and contrasts their **perspective** with the **people** that live on the Eggs. This comparison turns the **inhabitants** of the Eggs into **"wingless"** creatures and suggests that **Long Island** itself is a **safe nest** away from the **violent greed** and **immorality** of **New York**.

2) The Eggs are superficially **similar** — both are home to the **very wealthy**. However, West Egg is **"less fashionable"** than East Egg because of the **different sources** of the residents' **wealth**.

3) Nick decides that this **distinction** is **"bizarre and not a little sinister"** because it is designed to **discriminate families** with 'old money' from those with 'new money'.

Clocks symbolise a **Confusion** about **Time**

1) For **Gatsby**, his **reunion** with Daisy is the **event** around which his **time turns** — he's **"waited five years"**, and after she enters his house he runs down **"like an over-wound clock"**. Clocks are an **important symbol** during the **reunion**:

- Gatsby **leans** too hard against a **clock** when he finally sees Daisy. This symbolises that because he has been **waiting** so long to see her, he has put a lot of **pressure** on their eventual meeting.
- He apologises as if it had **"smashed in pieces on the floor"**. They **"all believed for a moment"** that it had actually **broken**, which could reflect their **willingness** to **accept** Gatsby's **destruction** of **time** and his attempt to **revise history**.

2) The **'broken'** clock indicates how the **passage** of **time** has been **perceived differently** by **different characters**. Daisy is vague about the **"many years"** that have passed since she last saw Gatsby. It's clear that time has passed more **slowly** for Gatsby who has counted **"five years next November"** exactly.

Everything **Represents** something, except for the **Books** — they're **Real**

1) In a world of **superficial appearances**, everything seems to **fall short** of what it **appears** to be.

2) Even Gatsby's **library** is **"panelled with carved English Oak"** to make his house **appear** more like the older **mansions** of the **established families**. This is an early hint that there is something **unreal** about Gatsby's house and life.

3) Fitzgerald uses **Owl Eyes** to suggest that Gatsby's **life** is a **theatrical front**, designed to **impress**. Owl Eyes is surprised when he finds out that Gatsby's **library** is full of **"absolutely real"** books. Instead of considering Gatsby as a **reader**, he congratulates him for his **"realism"**, as if Gatsby is a **theatrical designer** (see p.10).

4) It is **significant** that Gatsby's **books** are the only thing about his **created persona** that are **"absolutely real"**:

Novels are **fictional accounts** so books traditionally **symbolise unreality**. However, the book that Owl Eyes selects is a **non-fiction** travel guide — in a world of **fake appearances** the books represent **'reality'**.

Practice Questions

Q1 Explain the significance of Tom's car with respect to class and power.

Q2 How does Fitzgerald use imagery and symbolism to highlight the differences between East Egg and West Egg?

Q3 Choose a symbol from the novel. Explain how Fitzgerald uses it to represent three different things in different chapters.

"On the green Sound, stagnant in the heat, one small sail crawled slowly"

Oh boy, oh boy — this novel's steaming hot. Fitzgerald sets it at the height of summer, escalating events in line with the rising temperature. The uncomfortable weather is a sign of coming trouble, while all the symbols point to the source of the trouble.

Social Context

Fitzgerald coined the term 'Jazz Age' to describe boomtime America, an era which he criticised in his novels...

'The Great Gatsby' is all about Life in the 'Jazz Age'

1) *The Great Gatsby* is set in 1922, four years after the end of the **First World War**. This **period** after the war became known as '**The Roaring Twenties**', the '**Jazz Age**' or the '**Golden Years**' because of the **boom** in the economy:

> • The war put **pressure** on **industry** to keep America **ahead** — the country needed more **advanced weaponry** and **cheaper food** production. **Production rates increased** and **technology** became **more sophisticated**. This meant that **American industry** and the **economy** were **boosted** when the war ended in **1918**.
>
> • After the war there was more employment in the **expanded industries** and household **incomes increased**.

2) Along with **economic changes** came **major social** and **cultural changes**. Women had more **independence** and were able to **vote**, and they wanted a **new image** to reflect their **new lifestyle**.

3) **Fashion** and **architecture** changed quickly and dramatically — **women** started to dress in straight, low-waisted '**flapper**' dresses and **buildings** were designed according to **decorative 'Art Deco'** aesthetics.

4) The **pessimistic tone** of the novel suggests that Fitzgerald thought that the **boom** couldn't **last**. He was **right** — in 1929 the American **stock market crashed**. The resulting **depression** lasted until the **start of World War Two** in 1939.

5) Fitzgerald was part of the '**lost generation**' — this was a **generation** who **came of age during** the First World War. When the war had **finished**, people felt **restless** — the war had **defined their lives** and now they **lacked direction**.

The 1920s was a Decade of Consumption

1) **Post-war wealth** combined with wartime advances in technology. **American industry** began to develop **new** and **exciting products** such as **cars**, **refrigerators** and **radios**.

2) American families began to **earn more** and **buy more**. America became a nation of **early consumerism**.

3) **Advertisers** were suddenly in great demand to **promote** all the new **products** being created.

> **Advertising**
>
> **Advertising billboards** were introduced in the **mid 19th century**, and by the 1920s **advertising** was **everywhere**. **Jingles** started to appear on **commercial radio** after **1923** and companies like 'Burma Shave' started to put up **roadside signs** with **funny**, rhyming slogans in **1925**.

4) **Finance companies loaned** people **money** to buy the things that **advertising** had made seem so **attractive**. This landed people in **debt**. **High consumption** levels kept the **American economy healthy**, but **trapped** individuals in **debt**.

> Before becoming a novelist, Fitzgerald worked for a brief time as a copywriter for a New York advertising agency. His experience there may have made Fitzgerald realise the potency of advertising and its control over people's lives.

Not Everyone made their Money Legally

1) Not everyone made their **money** in **industry**. Some were selling **alcohol**, working with the **mafia** or **gambling**.

> **Bootlegging**
>
> • In **1919** a **law** was passed in America that made it **illegal** to **manufacture**, **sell** or **transport alcohol**. This was known as **prohibition**.
>
> • Some people, including **gangsters**, started to **sell** alcohol to **secret bars** called 'speakeasies' at a **great profit**. These traders became known as '**bootleggers**' because they originally **hid bottles** in their boots.

2) Fitzgerald weaves **real news stories** into Gatsby's backstory. Gatsby's involvement with **Wolfshiem** puts him right on the edge of a real and dangerous **underworld** of **gambling** and **gangster violence**.

> **Gambling**
>
> • **Wolfshiem** talks about '**Rosy**' **Rosenthal** who was **shot** by gangsters. This was a **real event** — the gambler **Herman Rosenthal** was shot in 1912 at the request of **corrupt policemen**.
>
> • Wolfshiem himself seems to be based on the **real-life gambler**, **Arnold Rothstein**, who was rumoured to have fixed the **World Series**, a major league baseball championship, in 1919.

Social Context

High Immigration Levels provoked Prejudice and caused Unrest

1) In *The Great Gatsby* the **main characters** are all **white, wealthy Americans**. However, characters like **Wolfshiem**, **Michaelis** and the **young black people** in the **limousine** (see p.59) remind the reader that other **ethnic groups** existed.

2) Thousands of **immigrants** arrived in America in the **19th century** to follow the 'American Dream'. Many of these immigrants arrived at **Ellis Island**, just off Manhattan, and decided to stay in **New York** and the surrounding areas.

3) The high concentration of **immigrants** led to **tension** between **different** groups. The **older** and more **established immigrants** had come from **northern Europe** and now identified themselves as **American**. This **naturalised** group was **uncomfortable** with the **arrival** of **new immigrants** from **southern** and **eastern Europe**.

Immigration Tensions

In **1924**, the **Immigration Act** was passed, which **restricted** the number of **southern** and **eastern Europeans** moving to the USA and completely **prohibited** immigration from much of **Asia**.

> **Prejudice** against 'new' immigrants was **common**. This is reflected in **Nick's representation** of the **Jewish** character, **Wolfshiem**, and **Tom Buchanan's nervousness** about the levels of immigration affecting the lives of the "**Nordics**".

New immigrants wait to be checked and have their papers processed on Ellis Island, New York, 1902.

4) **Racism** was **widespread**. Despite the **Slavery Abolition Act of 1833**, **African Americans** were still treated as **second-class citizens**.

America had seen Several Money-Making Booms

1) America's **east** and **west coasts** had very different **reputations**. The **West** was seen as a **frontier land** of **hard, physical work**. The **East** was connected with **fast living, financial gain** and **corrupt businessmen**.

2) Both the **east** and **west coasts** of America have seen **booms** as people arrived to achieve the '**American Dream**':

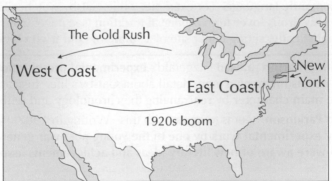

West Coast

In the **19th century** the American 'Gold Rush' started a huge **migration of workers** over to the **west side** of America in search of a **quick fortune**.

The Gold Rush

West Coast

East Coast

New York

1920s boom

East Coast

After WW1 people in the **east** started to **profit** from the **post-war banking boom**. During the 1920s, the east coast boomed, **economically** and in **population size**.

3) In *The Great Gatsby*, **Dan Cody followed** in the **wake** of the **gold rush**, and took part in "**every rush for metal since seventy-five**", mining **silver** in **Nevada** and **copper** in **Montana**. Nick pursues a career in "**bonds**" — **like** the **gold-diggers** who headed **west** in search of fortune, he **heads east** in search of **banking success**.

Practice Questions

Q1 Do you consider *The Great Gatsby* to be a political novel? Consider the topics of race, immigration and property as they are discussed by the novel's characters in your answer.

Q2 What role does the theme of prohibition play in the novel?

"a new generation dedicated... to the fear of poverty and the worship of success"

Fitzgerald emerged as the voice of a generation, and he was very well paid for it — at the height of his fame he made around fifty thousand dollars for a short story (in today's money). He celebrated by jumping into fountains and buying a life raft of champagne.

Critical Interpretations

Fitzgerald told his editor that he wanted his book to be a "consciously artistic achievement". No pressure, then...

Critics had High Expectations of 'The Great Gatsby'

1) Fitzgerald's first two novels were very popular with the American public. *This Side of Paradise* and *The Beautiful and Damned* both sold between **forty** and **fifty thousand** copies in their **first year** of publication. *The Great Gatsby* **only sold** around **half** that amount in 1925, the year it was published.

2) His earlier novels were also **highly praised** by **critics**, but *The Great Gatsby* was considered a **disappointment**. The magazine *New York World* said the book was a "**dud**".

3) **H.L. Mencken**, an **influential critic** writing for the *Baltimore Evening Sun* in 1925, **wasn't impressed** with the novel:

> **Early Critical Reviews**
>
> - Mencken commented on the "**charm and beauty of the writing**", but **criticised** the **lifelessness** of some of the characters: "**Only Gatsby himself genuinely lives and breathes. The rest are mere marionettes**".
>
> - In some ways, Mencken's review suggests that Fitzgerald **achieved** his **aims**. Fitzgerald had written to his publisher in early 1925 to say that he'd **redrafted** the novel, which had "**brought Gatsby to life**".
>
> - But, Fitzgerald wrote that he set out to write "**something** *new* — something extraordinary**", a "**consciously artistic achievement**" — Mencken's review suggests he **didn't achieve** this.

Some Readers thought that 'The Great Gatsby' was a Modern Novel

1) When *The Great Gatsby* was **published**, many **early reviewers** commented on the novel's **new style**.

2) The poet T.S. Eliot was **impressed** by the novel, writing in 1925 "**it seems to me to be the first step that American fiction has taken since Henry James**". **T.S. Eliot** was **congratulating** Fitzgerald on taking the **older 'realist' style**, and bringing it **up-to-date** to meet the expectations of the **modernist reader**. For more on '**modernism**', see p.48.

> **Realism**
>
> **Henry James** was a **19th-century** author who used **realistic** characters and scenarios to represent **contemporary life** — James was a '**literary realist**'. Fitzgerald didn't write in a **realist style**, but he used **elements** of **Realism** to **contrast** with his **Romantic language**. For example, while Gatsby watches Daisy's house in Chapter 8, he adopts the **role** of the **chivalrous lover** from **Medieval tradition** (see pages 20 and 48). However, Daisy and Tom are presented more **realistically**, sitting either site of a "**plate of cold fried chicken**" and "**two bottles of ale**".

3) In 1925 the novelist **Edith Wharton praised** Fitzgerald's **experimental presentation** of Gatsby's character. Wharton thought that **traditional** novels might give more detail about Gatsby's life. Instead, Fitzgerald purposely **clouds** the reader's **vision** of the **main character** by **rearranging** the **chronology** and **withholding information**.

4) A recent critic, **Kathleen Parkinson**, seems to **agree** with this. Writing in 1987, Parkinson says that *The Great Gatsby* is a "**consciously experimental work by one of the young post-war generation of American writers who visited Europe and were aware of new literary ideas and achievements associated with Modernism**".

Other Readers seemed to think it was more Traditional

1) **Gertrude Stein** was an **American writer** living in **Paris** in the early 20th century, when **modernism** was **flourishing**.

2) In 1925 Stein said that *The Great Gatsby* was "**creating the contemporary world**" — she thought Fitzgerald **captured** the **mood** of the **times**. She **compared** *The Great Gatsby* to the novels of **William Makepeace Thackeray**, a 19th-century author:

> **Satire**
>
> **Thackeray** was an author famous for writing **critical** and **satirical** novels about the **excesses** of **19th-century society**. Like *The Great Gatsby* his novels give the reader **no clear lesson** — they just present the **world** as Thackeray **saw it**.

Gertrude Stein

3) Stein seems to be saying that Fitzgerald is doing something **new** for a **new audience**, but using **established writing methods**. In *The Great Gatsby,* Fitzgerald mixes **Romantic language**, **realist speech** and **satirical tones**, which are all **traditional elements**.

Critical Interpretations

In the 1940s there was a Fitzgerald Revival

1) When Fitzgerald **died** in **1940**, **obituaries** and **reviews** praised Fitzgerald's writing and sparked **interest** in his work.

2) As the decade progressed, the *The Great Gatsby* began to be taken **more seriously** as a **great work** of literature, and the **novel** started to be seen as a **self-portrait** of **Fitzgerald**:

William Troy

William Troy's article, 'Scott Fitzgerald — the Authority of Failure' was published in 1945. Troy argued that Fitzgerald used **Nick** and **Gatsby** to **represent** two **forces** in his own life — **"intelligent and responsible"** versus **"dream-ridden romantic"**.

This suggests that Nick grows in self-awareness during Gatsby's downfall — their progress mirrors one another. However, critics such as R.W. Stallman (see below), thought that Nick learns nothing from his experience.

In the 1950s Gatsby turned into a Myth

1) In the **1950s** critics were influenced by **'New Criticism'** to look beyond Fitzgerald's own life to study the novel closely for **symbolism** and **universal meaning**.

2) At the same time, other 1950s critics looked more **broadly** at Gatsby as a **character** who belonged to the **society** and **culture** of his time.

New Criticism

New Critics looked at the text **very closely**. Instead of considering **context**, such as the **author's life** or the **politics** of the time, they read the novel on its **own** to look at its **formal techniques**.

Lionel Trilling

Lionel Trilling's book *The Liberal Imagination* was published in 1951. He argued that Gatsby's **dreams** are central to his life, but that his **dreams** are kept in check by his **'power'** to **achieve** them. Trilling concludes that because **Gatsby** is caught between **'power'** and **'dream'** he represents **"America itself"**, because America is **split** between the **fantasy** of the **'American Dream'** and the reality of the **individual's power** to run his own life.

R.W. Stallman

In his essay, **'Gatsby and the Hole in Time'** (1955), **Stallman** imagines Gatsby as **"a modern Icarus"**. In **Ancient Greek** myth, Icarus was a man whose **ambition** to **fly** too high led to his **own downfall**.

In the 1960s critics analysed Fitzgerald's representation of Ethnic Minorities

1) **1960s critics** commented on Fitzgerald's treatment of **Jewish** and **African American** characters in *The Great Gatsby* and the fact that he doesn't mention the existence of **Native Americans** who lived in America **before** the **settlers**.

2) Fitzgerald's portrayal of **Meyer Wolfshiem** turns him into a **caricature** of **offensive Jewish stereotypes** — Wolfshiem's **accent**, small **eyes** and **corrupt gambling habits** are all designed to make him seem **comic** and **untrustworthy**.

3) Robert Forrey's essay *Negroes in the Fiction of F. Scott Fitzgerald* (1965) criticises the portrayal of **black Americans**:

Robert Forrey

Forrey writes that **Nick** is **surprised** by the idea that **black Americans** could be **successful** or **wealthy** themselves. For example, in Chapter 4 Nick says he **"laughed aloud"** when he saw **"two bucks and a girl"** in a **limousine**. Forrey notes that Fitzgerald uses **"disparaging"** language to describe black Americans, using words like **'buck'**, a **trading term** from America's history of **slavery**.

Practice Questions

Q1 How does Fitzgerald incorporate elements of Realism and Romanticism into *The Great Gatsby*?

Q2 Do you agree with H.L. Mencken's assessment that Fitzgerald's characters are unrealistic "marionettes"?

Q3 To what extent do you consider Fitzgerald's representation of ethnicity to be a product of its time?

"something extraordinary and beautiful and simple + intricately patterned"

The Moderns were an exciting bunch. They had a lot on their plate though — from the war recovery to recovery from bad reviews, it was a tough time. And just like Gatsby's party-goers, they didn't always know how best to cope with it all. Poor old Moderns.

Critical Interpretations

These interpretations are ordered by decade but the debates continued into the following years...

In the **1970s Feminist** critics looked at the roles of the **Women** in the novel

1) The 1970s **feminist critics** started to question the way most novels **prioritise** the **male experience** of **life**.

2) Some **feminist critics** looked at the way **Fitzgerald** described the **physical appearance** of Daisy:

> Joan S. Korenman
>
> Korenman's article **'"Only her hairdresser...": Another Look at Daisy Buchanan'** (1975) claims that Fitzgerald **purposely** keeps the colour of Daisy's hair **ambiguous**. For **example**:
>
> > Daisy compares her hair to her daughter's **"old yellowy hair"**. At other times her **"dark shining hair"** is said to lie like a **"dash of blue paint across her cheek"**.
>
> Korenman says that the **ambiguity** lets Daisy symbolise both **"the fair and the dark women of romantic literature"**. **Traditional stereotypes** cast **fair-haired** women as **innocent** and **dark-haired** women as **dangerous temptresses**.

If Daisy is both **light** and **dark-haired**, she **symbolises** Gatsby's **ideal** and his **downfall**.

3) Other **feminist critics** looked at how **Fitzgerald** gave **other objects** a **female form**:

> Judith Fetterley
>
> • In Fetterley's book, *The Resisting Reader: A Feminist Approach to American Fiction* (1977), she argues that **"American literature is male"** — it is written from a **male perspective** for the **male reader**.
>
> • Fetterley notices that Fitzgerald gives the **American coast** a **female identity**, with a **"green breast"**. **Lionel Trilling** claimed that Gatsby was **"America itself"** (see p.59) but Fetterley claims that **"it is Daisy herself who is America"**. Fetterley argues that **women** are like the **'American Dream'** because they are **fantasised about**, but **blamed** for **male characters' failure** to achieve their **dreams**.

In the **1980s Marxist Critics** saw the novel as a **Social Commentary**

1) **Marxist theory** is concerned with **capital** (**money** or **products of labour**) and **'capitalist' societies**. Critics who use Marxism to **analyse** a **novel** will look at the characters' **relationships** with **class**, **money**, **work** and **each other**.

2) For example, when Nick refers to the **"floating rounds of cocktails"** in Chapter 3, the word **"floating"** could suggest that Nick **ignores** the fact that Gatsby's hired **staff** are holding up the trays. A **Marxist analysis** of Nick's **language** suggests he overlooks the **existence** of the **working class**.

3) The critic Ross Posnock argued that **everything** in *The Great Gatsby*, including **people**, is turned into an **object**.

> Ross Posnock
>
> In his essay **'"A New World, Material Without Being Real": Fitzgerald's Critique of Capitalism in *The Great Gatsby*'** (1984) Posnock argues that people in Gatsby's society are so **obsessed** with **material wealth** that they treat each other as **objects**. This **stops** Gatsby from being able to **love** — he sees Daisy as a **prize** he can **'buy'**.

4) In **capitalist societies** people collect **objects** and **capital** to increase their **social status**. In this way, objects become **status symbols** (see p.54) and take on a **symbolic value** in addition to their **financial worth**.

> Nick notices that Gatsby has a collection of **"enchanted objects"** that includes the **green light**, and **possessions** that he sees as **symbolically** as well as financially **important**:
>
> > Gatsby's wardrobe is full of clothing made from **"thick silk"** and **expensive dyes** like Indian blue, piled like **"bricks in stacks a dozen high"**. This makes his clothes sound like a **heavy defensive wall** or like **gold bars** stacked in a **bank vault**. His clothes help to protect his **status**.

Critical Interpretations

In the **1990s Postmodernism** looked at Modernism in a new light

1) In the 1990s, critics began to take a **postmodern** view of *The Great Gatsby*. Postmodernist critics argued that there should be **no differentiation** between **high culture** (things like **opera** and **literature**) and **low culture** (pop music, cartoons and advertising). They were interested in *The Great Gatsby* because Fitzgerald seems to **mix high** and **low culture** by combining references to both **Romantic language** and **modern technology** (see p.48).

2) Postmodernist critics are also interested in **commercial spaces** e.g. **marketplaces**, **advertising billboards** and **hotels**:

> ### Ronald Berman
> In his book ***The Great Gatsby and Modern Times***, published in 1994, Berman looked at Fitzgerald's use of **commercial** and **media references** in the novel. He writes that the **characters** in *The Great Gatsby* have **closer relationships** with **"published, advertised, and perceived images"** than they do with **each other**. He refers to the fact that **Wilson** can't tell the **difference** between **God** and the **"gigantic"** eyes of **T.J. Eckleburg's billboard**, and that Nick recognises **Jordan's expression** from a **"rotogravure" image** from the **newspapers** and remembers her later as a **"good illustration"**. Fitzgerald's characters are so used to seeing **advertising** and **media images** that they can't **separate** them from **reality**.

3) Postmodernists **rejected** the idea of **one big reality** — they said that **no single narrative** could explain all of **human history** and **experience**. Postmodernists explored **plural narratives** told by **multiple voices** in novels such as *The Great Gatsby*, which uses a '**choric voice**' (see p.49), and the **voice** of an **unreliable narrator** (see p.26) who **borrows** information from other **sources**. Because of this, the reader is **never sure** of the whole '**truth**'.

The Great Gatsby still **Appeals** to **Readers Today**

1) In 1940, a ***New York Times*** editorial claimed that *The Great Gatsby* was "**not a book for the ages**". It was seen as a novel that **belonged** to the 1920s and wouldn't be **appreciated** by later readers.

2) However, in 2008 Sara Rimer wrote an article for the ***New York Times***, which argued that *The Great Gatsby* is a text that **students** still **identify** with:

> ### Sara Rimer
> In her article, '**Gatsby's Green Light Beckons a New Set of Strivers**', Rimer argued that Gatsby's "**green light**" has come to **symbolise** the **aspirations** of many **young people**. Gatsby's character is like that of a **celebrity** who has managed to follow a '**dream**' to build a **successful career**. However, Gatsby's story is told with a "**level of honesty**" that turns the novel into a "**cautionary tale**". Rimer argues that this balanced message is especially relevant to America's **school-age immigrants** who come to America to get a **better education** and **improve** their **future**.

3) While a **film version** of *The Great Gatsby*, due out in 2012, was in development, the director, **Baz Luhrmann**, said that he thought it was a **good time** to remake *The Great Gatsby* because the "**story of *Gatsby* speaks so directly to what we have just gone through**". Luhrmann may have been referring to the way the novel's **themes** of **excess** and **loss resonate** with today's readers, who have dealt with **war** and economic recession in **recent years**.

4) The novel's **broader themes** of **love**, **ambition** and the '**American Dream**' mean that modern readers can still find new ways to **connect** with the **story**.

Practice Questions

Q1 Discuss the presentation of women in *The Great Gatsby*.

Q2 Does Gatsby love Daisy as a person or as an object he'd like to possess?

Q3 How relevant do you think *The Great Gatsby* is to readers' lives today?

"It was when curiosity about Gatsby was at its highest..."

From the 1940s obituaries to the 1970s feminist "resistance" reading, and even to the Postmodernists, 'The Great Gatsby' has really been put through its paces. By 1974, more than 2400 university courses in America had 'The Great Gatsby' on their reading lists.

Writing About 'The Great Gatsby'

Whether or not you think that 'The Great Gatsby' really is great, or average, or bad, there's a surefire way to make your essays great. There's a simple but effective structure that you can follow in order to do well...

Use a *Plan* to *Structure* your *Argument*

1) **Before** you **start planning**, pick out the **key words** in the **question** so that you can **focus** on the most **important points**.

2) Once you've **worked out** exactly what the question's **asking**, you can start to **plan your argument**.

3) The **best essays** follow a **clear structure**:

> • Your **introduction** should set out your **argument clearly** and **effectively** — it's the reader's **first impression** of your essay, so make sure it's a **good one**.
>
> • Each **paragraph** should consider **one key point** of your **argument**. Don't try to cram everything into a couple of long paragraphs — you should consider **each point properly**.
>
> • Every **paragraph** needs to **develop your answer** and each one should **follow on clearly** from the one before — this will make your argument more **persuasive**.
>
> • Your **conclusion** should **summarise** your **argument clearly** and **concisely**. Give a **final answer** to the **question** and **your personal response** to the text.

4) Plan your **argument** by making a **list** of **all** your **points** and the **evidence** that you're going to use to **back up** each one — this means that your argument will be **supported** all the way through.

5) Work out the **best order** to **tackle** your points so that the essay **flows naturally**. Try **linking** your **paragraphs** by placing **similar topics** next to each other — you could use **bullet points**, **tables** or **spider diagrams** to organise the ideas in your plan.

Use *Quotes* to *Back Up* your *Points*

Quoting from both the **novel** and **critics** is a good way of **backing up** your **argument**:

> If you're quoting from the **novel**, **analyse** the quotes, rather than simply **listing** them. Tell the reader what the quote **shows** and how it **supports your argument**. Avoid using **long quotes** with lots of **ellipses**.
>
> > Nick thinks that Gatsby's dream was unobtainable. He concludes that "the green light... year by year recedes before us... So we beat on, boats against the current, borne back ceaselessly into the past".
>
> > Nick believes that the green light represents the "orgastic future" that Gatsby longed for. However, he could never achieve it, because we are all like "boats against the current", constantly pulled back "into the past".

> Be **selective** if you're quoting a **critic** — it shows your reader that you're using a critic's argument to make a **valid point**. It also shows that you **understand** that it's the **argument** that's **important**, and not that you can **remember** lots of **quotes**.
>
> > Joan S. Korenman argues that Daisy's ambiguous hair colour "reflects a fundamental duality in Daisy herself, her simultaneous embodiment of traits associated with the fair and the dark women of romantic literature".
>
> > Joan S. Korenman argues that Daisy's ambiguous hair colour allows Fitzgerald to give her the mixed traits of "the fair and the dark women of romantic literature". In this way, Daisy can be seen as an innocent victim and a manipulative seducer.
>
> You need to make **critical quotes part** of your argument rather than simply using them **as your argument**. Don't be afraid to **challenge** critical views with your **own opinions**. You can **evaluate** the **strengths** and **weaknesses** of **critical approaches** as you **develop** your **answer**. Remember that if you're writing an **undergraduate essay** you'll need to **reference** your critics **properly**.

Writing About 'The Great Gatsby'

There are **Five Key Things** to **Think About** when **Writing** an **Essay**

CULTURAL AND HISTORICAL CONTEXT	Look at the **influences** that **shaped** the **text**, the **author's opinions** and **writing style**. Consider how the context would have **affected** the **audience** it was written for. Have a look at **pages 48-51** and **56-58** for an **idea** of what to look for.
ANALYSING FORM AND STRUCTURE	Look at the **genre** (e.g. whether it's a **tragedy** or a **comedy**) and its **form** (e.g. a **novel** instead of a **poem** or **play**) and look at how they've **affected** the way the text is **written**. When looking at the **structure**, you should **consider** how the **plot unfolds**, and how the text is **shaped** by **chapters** and **paragraphs**, as well as the **setting** (see **pages 46-47**).
CLOSE ANALYSIS OF LANGUAGE	Look at **short extracts** or **paragraphs** to **analyse** the **language** that the author uses to **create certain effects**. This could involve looking at things like **slang words**, **tone** and **adjectives**.
A RANGE OF CRITICAL OPINIONS	Consider **different critical approaches** to the text, **analyse** their **arguments** and decide if you **agree** or **disagree** with them. **Critical opinion** is a useful way to **support** your arguments.
THE RELATIONSHIP BETWEEN DIFFERENT TEXTS	Look at **other works** that share the **same form** or **themes** and see how **other authors** approach them (see **pages 48-49**). It's also **helpful** to look at **other works** by the **same author**.

A-Level Examiners Look at Four Main Skills...

These Assessment Objectives are for A-Level English Literature only.

To get **top marks** at **A-level** you need to make sure that you show that you **understand** and **meet** the **assessment objectives**. Assessment objectives are **helpful little clues** that tell you what the **examiners** want to see in **your work**:

1 **Assessment Objective 1 — AO1**

You need to write **clearly**, **accurately** and with **good spelling**. Your work must show **creative thought**, **answer the question**, and be **backed up** with a good **knowledge** of the **text**. You should use **technical terms** where it's **appropriate** (e.g. personification, allegory, allusion).

2 **Assessment Objective 2 — AO2**

You need to **analyse in detail** how **structure**, **form** and **language** create **meanings** in the text.

3 **Assessment Objective 3 — AO3**

You need to **compare** and **contrast different texts** with one another. You should give a **reasonable personal response** to the different texts as well as taking into account **other interpretations**.

4 **Assessment Objective 4 — AO4**

You need to **understand** how **context** might have **influenced** the text. **Explain** the **impact** of the **historical**, **cultural** and **literary** context on the **author** and the **audience**.

"Show me a hero and I'll write you a tragedy" — F. Scott Fitzgerald...

This explains why Fitzgerald didn't do very well when he tried his hand at screenwriting. Imagine a movie where Bond gets his licence to kill revoked or where Spider-Man gets caught in a web of lies or where Harry Potter doesn't make any money... Sounds terrible.

Writing About 'The Great Gatsby'

You might be writing about 'The Great Gatsby' for your exam or your coursework.
This page deals mostly with an exam-type essay question, but it'll be helpful for coursework too.

Pick out the Key Words in the Question

By discussing a good range of characters, rather than focusing on one or two, you can show a good knowledge of the text (AO1).

What do you think of the view that there are no characters in *The Great Gatsby* that the reader can sympathise with?

Think about different critical views that could be used e.g. feminist critics who suggest a more sympathetic reading of Daisy (AO3).

You could talk about how the readers' sympathy for characters might have changed over time (AO3/AO4).

You can analyse in detail how Nick, as the narrator, uses language to create sympathetic or critical images of other characters. You could also explore what Fitzgerald is trying to achieve and how he uses language to do it (AO2).

Introduce your Argument in the Introduction

You might **start** like this:

This shows an understanding of the view that none of the characters are sympathetic, while also introducing a valid reason for disagreeing with that view.

The majority of the characters in 'The Great Gatsby' are undeniably selfish and materialistic, and Fitzgerald's portrayal encourages the reader to judge them. However, although each character is deeply flawed, these flaws make them vulnerable and unhappy. Many readers can relate to the characters' weaknesses. This suggests that Fitzgerald intended the reader to criticise the characters, but sympathise with them too.

Referring to the terms used in the question shows your answer is focused.

This introduction is **good** because it **sets the scene** for the rest of the essay — the **reader** knows that the essay will look at **why** many of the characters are **unpleasant**, but also explore **reasons why** readers will still **sympathise** with them.

Make your First Paragraph about the most Important Point

The **first paragraph** should **expand on** the **key point** from the **introduction** more **fully**:

A key example of the reader's simultaneous dislike of and sympathy for the characters is provided by the relationship between Gatsby and Daisy. He is captivated by the "bought luxury" that surrounds her, and she only shows real emotion when she's admiring his possessions, "'They're such beautiful shirts,' she sobbed". This shows that their love is inextricably linked to materialism, making it hard for the reader to sympathise with the romance. However, Gatsby's loneliness as he waits for Daisy, and Daisy's feeling of being "utterly abandoned" are portrayed poignantly. The characters' unhappiness elicits pity from the readers, even though this unhappiness was arguably brought about by their own materialistic values.

These short quotes show good textual knowledge and help support the argument (AO1).

This gives **textual evidence** that the characters' **materialism** shouldn't **stop** the reader from **sympathising** with them, so it **makes sense** to go on to explain **why** Fitzgerald might **want** his readers to **sympathise** with the **characters**.

The fact that Daisy is still an appealing character, despite being shallow, reflects Fitzgerald's own confused feelings about the 'Jazz Age'. Fitzgerald was simultaneously attracted to and repulsed by the way society had embraced consumerism. Daisy is frequently associated with light, for example "the last sunshine fell... upon her glowing face", which makes her seem pure and warm, but she's also identified with material wealth: she is "gleaming like silver", which emphasises her materialism. This mix of glamour and corruption exists throughout 'The Great Gatsby', and it encourages the reader to criticise some aspects of the characters, but to sympathise with them nevertheless.

This is good because it shows knowledge of the novel's historical context, and gives an example of Fitzgerald's own views (AO4).

This paragraph provides a clear **interpretation** of **Fitzgerald's intentions** with **textual** evidence and **context**.

Writing About 'The Great Gatsby'

Consider a Variety of Critical Viewpoints

Use **critics** to **support** your argument, but don't be afraid to **challenge** their opinions if you **disagree**:

> Some critics argue that Gatsby sees Daisy as a prize, and not as a woman he can love. For example, Ross Posnock argues that Gatsby's dreams are too materialistic to be inspiring. However, I would argue that the focus of Gatsby's character is his ability to hope for and strive towards better things — he believes in "the green light, the orgastic future". This act of hoping is something that most readers will have experienced, and this makes Gatsby a very sympathetic character.

Using individual critics is good — you don't have to quote them directly, but make sure you get their arguments right (AO3).

This is **good**, but rather than just **stating** a critic's opinion, you need to **develop** it and **analyse** it yourself:

> Posnock's argument misses the deliberate ambiguity of Gatsby's dreams, which are both pathetic and admirable. Although it is difficult for the reader to sympathise with Gatsby's pursuit of Daisy, which is essentially a dream of empty materialism, they can admire and sympathise with Gatsby's "extraordinary gift for hope".

This engages with the critics' arguments by explaining what you think is missing from their interpretations (AO3).

This **engages** with the critics and **applies** their views to the **text**.

Think about Readings of the Novel at Different Times

Because *The Great Gatsby* is a novel 'of its time', it's useful to consider how **readings** of the text have **changed**.

This shows good knowledge of the context the novel was written in (AO4).

This provides close language analysis of the text that is relevant to the question (AO2).

> Some of the characters' racist beliefs make them less sympathetic. For example, Nick mocks Wolfshiem's "expressive nose" and the way that he pronounces connection as "gonnegtion", turning him into a caricature of a Jew. Whereas a modern reader may find this offensive, readers in 1925, when Fitzgerald was writing, would probably have thought this was acceptable. Whilst Nick's racial stereotypes are insulting but not aggressive, in contrast, Tom is portrayed as an unintelligent racist, who thinks that white people have "produced all the things that go to make civilization — oh, science and art, and all that." The use of a pause, as shown by the hyphen, suggests he's hesitant, and the word "oh" suggests that he's struggling to find the right words. Finally, the phrase "and all that" suggests that he can't remember the argument, or think of any further examples. Fitzgerald present Tom's racism as ignorant and ridiculous, which makes him a less sympathetic character.

By considering how **different periods** have affected the novel's **interpretation** you're forced to **consider** the **context** of *The Great Gatsby*, so it's a good way to make sure you pick up **extra marks**.

Your Conclusion should Concisely Summarise your Argument

The conclusion doesn't need to introduce any **new ideas**, but it should put forward a **balanced answer** to the question:

This is good because it directly answers the question.

> Although each character in 'The Great Gatsby' is flawed, this does not mean that there are no characters that the reader can sympathise with. The power of 'The Great Gatsby' lies in the ambiguous nature of the characterisation. Just like Nick, many readers will be "simultaneously enchanted and repelled" by the characters — criticising their selfish behaviour while admiring their glamorous lifestyle, and sympathising with their emotional turmoil. This reflects the moral confusion of America in the 1920s. Fitzgerald's realistic portrayal, refusing to present characters as wholly 'sympathetic' or 'unsympathetic', allows readers to engage with the characters while remaining aware of their immorality.

This conclusion is **concise** and provides a **reasonable argument** that **answers** the **question**.

Writing About 'The Great Gatsby'

Another type of question that you might be asked to answer is one that focuses on a short extract, passage or chapter from the novel. If this type of question's your poison, then this page is the antidote.

You might get a **Question** about a **Specific Part** of the **Novel**

1) Questions about a **specific part** of the novel are obvious to spot, but it's **less obvious** how to **start answering them**. They could ask about **any length** of extract ranging from a **few lines** to a **whole chapter**.

2) These questions might focus on a **specific aspect** of the extract, such as the **language** or **style**, or they might ask more **generally** about how Fitzgerald '**tells the story**' in that particular extract.

3) It's much **easier** to answer questions about specific aspects, as it gives you a **starting point** for your answer. As long as you **focus** on what the question is **asking you about**, you should do fine.

4) **General questions** are **harder** to answer because they don't give you much **guidance**. Some of the **things** you should consider are:

> * **Form** — Modern tragedy, love story, a novel about writing a novel.
> * **Structure** — Chronology (e.g. introduction with hindsight, flashbacks), different viewpoints.
> * **Language** — Imagery, symbolism, adjectives, colloquialisms, dialogue.
> * **Narrative Style** — First or third person, collective narratives, self-awareness.
> * **Setting** — The 'Jazz Age', weather, different places and what each place represents (e.g. East Egg represents old money, West Egg represents new money).

Think about **How** to **Structure** your **Answer** to an **Extract Question**

Below is an **example** of how you might **answer** a question about how Fitzgerald **tells the story** in **Chapter 3**. There's **no set way** to answer an **extract question** — this is just **one way** you could approach it.

1) Talk about the extract more **generally** to **begin with**, e.g. the **focus** of the extract and how it **fits in** with the novel:

This paragraph gives a general perspective on the chapter by exploring its structure and how that relates to the plot.

> Chapter 3 is the first time that Gatsby is introduced in person. By delaying Gatsby's introduction, Fitzgerald creates suspense and develops the mystery surrounding Gatsby's character. When Nick describes his meeting with Gatsby, Fitzgerald changes the narrative focus of the novel. Until Chapter 3, the novel is written entirely from Nick's perspective, but this is the first time that other voices are introduced. These new perspectives introduce outlandish rumours about Gatsby such as "he killed a man" and "he was a German spy" to further obscure the truth about Gatsby.

2) Then move on to explore **narrative style** and how it **affects** the **atmosphere**:

> There is a notable shift in narrative style in this chapter — Nick's voice changes from past tense to present tense for a page. He tells us that "The bar is in full swing... the air is alive... The lights grow brighter". This use of present tense makes the reader feel as if the party is still happening, drawing them in to the atmosphere of glamour and excitement.

This paragraph moves from a general discussion to a more specific exploration of the writing in the extract.

3) You can then **expand** on the **role** of **narrative techniques** to **develop** your **points further**:

> Nick's description of the party is initially romantic: the air is said to be "alive with chatter and laughter", they listen to "yellow cocktail music" and "the earth lurches away from the sun" as time speeds up for Nick. However, as he experiences the debauchery of the party Nick's descriptions become more focused and realistic. Nick draws attention to tensions in relationships, with one man talking to an actress with "curious intensity" while his wife tries to stop him, and numerous fights between women and "men said to be their husbands". This shift in tone reflects Nick's own confused feelings about the decadent lifestyle of the East and, on a broader scale, it also reflects Fitzgerald's mixed opinions about the 'Jazz Age'.

4) You should go on to look at **other aspects** such as **form**, **language** and **setting** in a **similar level** of **detail**.

Comparing 'The Great Gatsby'

'The Great Gatsby' addresses major themes in literature like hope, love and death, so it can easily be compared with different texts. If you're stuck for ideas, then this is the page for you... if not, then you're in the wrong place my friend.

You could **Compare** 'The Great Gatsby' with **Post-1920s Literature**

1) A good place to **start** is to look at how **ideas**, **attitudes** and **opinions** have **developed** since the 1920s. There are **two main ways** you could approach this:

> **You could look at...**
> - **Specific elements** (for example, how ideas about the **American Dream** have **changed** over **time**).
> - **More general issues** (for example, how **attitudes** towards **gender** and **race** have **changed**).

2) *The Great Gatsby* is **closely linked** with the **Jazz Age** in 1920s America. This period in American history had a **distinct culture** and **morality**, so it's easy to **draw comparisons** with **different cultures** and **different periods**.

DIFFERENT TIME PERIODS
- Recent **literature** has the **benefit** of looking back at the 1920s with **hindsight**. Authors who **write about** the **1920s** know that the economic prosperity **didn't last** and that everything changed with the 1929 **Wall Street Crash**. This knowledge will **affect** their **writing style** and **tone**.
- **Society** has **changed dramatically** since the 1920s. For example, views on **women's roles**, **marriage** and **alcohol** are **very different now**. This means there will be lots of **contrasts** to be made with texts that are set in a **later period** or in the **present day**.

DIFFERENT CULTURES
- *The Great Gatsby* is an obviously **American novel**, so there are clear **cultural differences** that can be **examined** by looking at works by authors of **different nationalities**. **Authors** of **different nationalities** might **relate** to their **setting** in a **different** way, or respond to issues of **morality** differently to Fitzgerald.
- You could compare Fitzgerald to American authors with a **different cultural background**, e.g. **race** or **class**, and discuss how their views on **American culture** are **different** and how they're **similar**.

3) Most of the **themes** in *The Great Gatsby*, such as **money**, **religion** and **gender** are still **relevant** in post-1920s literature, while **universal issues** like **love** and **death** can be studied in relation to most **novels**, **poems** or **plays**.

You could **Compare** 'The Great Gatsby' with **Other Literature**

If you're comparing *The Great Gatsby* with works by Fitzgerald's **contemporaries** or with **older pieces** of literature, your comparison might focus on **different aspects** than if you were comparing it with literature that was written **later**. E.g:

1) If you're studying a work by one of Fitzgerald's **contemporaries** e.g. Ernest Hemingway or T.S. Eliot, you could look at how they **presented the same period** and **addressed similar issues**. It might be interesting to consider how someone from a **different background** to Fitzgerald **experienced** the **'Jazz Age'**.

2) If you're comparing the novel with an **older piece** of literature you can look at the **presentation of shared themes** and how **attitudes and ideas** have **changed over time**. You could also consider **differences** in **styles** or **genres** e.g. Romanticism or Realism.

Some of Fitzgerald's short stories (e.g. 'The Diamond as Big as the Ritz' and 'The Cut-Glass Bowl') make a good comparison with 'The Great Gatsby' because they deal with similar themes, for example, the American Dream, wealth and appearances.

You could **Compare** 'The Great Gatsby' with **Poetry**

1) If you're comparing *The Great Gatsby* with a poem, you could focus on the **different requirements** of the two **forms** (**novel** and **poem**).

2) Because poems are generally a lot **shorter** than *The Great Gatsby*, you could **pick short extracts** from the novel that share **similar themes** to the poem but which provide a **good contrast** in terms of **language** and **style**.

3) You could consider **shared imagery** and how the two authors examine **similar ideas differently** in their works.

4) **Songs** and **song lyrics** play an **important part** in *The Great Gatsby*, and how Fitzgerald presents and uses these **sections** of the **novel** could provide an **interesting point** of **comparison** with any poem.

Key Quotes

This page is a gift from me to you... you've come this far, so you deserve it. Use this page for inspiration when you can't quite remember that all-important quote or you need some ideas for a theme-based 'The Great Gatsby' essay. Enjoy...

Important Quotes

Gatsby turned out all right at the end; it is what preyed on Gatsby, what foul dust floated in the wake of his dreams that temporarily closed out my interest in the abortive sorrows and shortwinded elations of men. (Ch.1)

"Whenever you feel like criticizing any one... just remember that all the people in this world haven't had the advantages that you've had." (Ch.1)

"I've had a very bad time, Nick, and I'm pretty cynical about everything." (Ch.1)

A valley of ashes — a fantastic farm where ashes grow like wheat into ridges and hills and grotesque gardens; where ashes take the forms of houses and chimneys and rising smoke and, finally, with a transcendent effort, of ash-grey men. (Ch.2)

I was within and without, simultaneously enchanted and repelled by the inexhaustible variety of life. (Ch.2)

It was one of those rare smiles with a quality of eternal reassurance in it. (Ch.3)

"Can't repeat the past?" he cried incredulously. "Why of course you can!" (Ch.6)

Jordan... unlike Daisy, was too wise ever to carry well-forgotten dreams from age to age. (Ch.7)

"They're a rotten crowd," I shouted across the lawn. "You're worth the whole damn bunch put together." (Ch.8)

Theme: Money and the American Dream

He stretched out his arms toward the dark water in a curious way... I glanced seaward — and distinguished nothing except a single green light (Ch.1)

There are loads of other important quotes — have a look at Section 3 for more quotes relating to themes.

The colossal significance of that light had now vanished forever... His count of enchanted objects had diminished by one. (Ch.5)

There must have been moments even that afternoon when Daisy tumbled short of his dreams... because of the colossal vitality of his illusion. (Ch.5)

"Her voice is full of money" (Ch.7)

I became aware of the old island here that flowered once for Dutch sailors' eyes — a fresh, green breast of the new world. Its vanished trees... had once pandered in whispers to the last and greatest of all human dreams (Ch.9)

Gatsby believed in the green light, the orgastic future that year by year recedes before us. It eluded us then, but that's no matter — tomorrow we will run faster, stretch out our arms further... And one fine morning — So we beat on, boats against the current, borne back ceaselessly into the past. (Ch.9)

Theme: Appearance and Reality

"Absolutely real — have pages and everything... they're absolutely real... This fella's a regular Belasco. It's a triumph. What thoroughness! What realism!" (Ch.3)

Dishonesty in a woman is a thing you never blame deeply (Ch.3)

Then it was all true. I saw the skins of tigers flaming in his palace on the Grand Canal (Ch.4)

Jay Gatsby... sprang from his Platonic conception of himself. (Ch.6)

It was a photograph of the house... He had shown it so often that I think it was more real to him now than the house itself. (Ch.9)

Key Quotes

Theme: Love and Relationships

"I married him because I thought he was a gentleman... I thought he knew something about breeding, but he wasn't fit to lick my shoe." (Ch.2)

"Daisy! Daisy! Daisy!" shouted Mrs. Wilson. "I'll say it whenever I want to! Daisy! Dai —" Making a short deft movement, Tom Buchanan broke her nose (Ch.2)

I liked to walk up Fifth Avenue and pick out romantic women from the crowd and imagine that in a few minutes I was going to enter into their lives, and no one would ever know or disapprove. (Ch.3)

I felt a haunting loneliness sometimes... wasting the most poignant moments of night and life. (Ch.3)

He kissed this girl, and forever wed his unutterable visions to her perishable breath (Ch.6)

She began to sob helplessly. "I did love him once — but I loved you too." (Ch.7)

They weren't happy... and yet they weren't unhappy either. There was an unmistakable air of natural intimacy (Ch.7)

"You said a bad driver was only safe until she met another bad driver? Well, I met another bad driver, didn't I?" (Ch.9)

Theme: Religion and Morality

A sense of the fundamental decencies is parcelled out unequally at birth. (Ch.1)

When I came back from the East last autumn I felt that I wanted the world to be in uniform and at a sort of moral attention forever (Ch.1)

Everyone suspects himself of at least one of the cardinal virtues, and this is mine: I am one of the few honest people that I have ever known. (Ch.3)

His mind would never romp again like the mind of God. (Ch.6)

He was a son of God — a phrase which, if it means anything, means just that — and he must be about His Father's business, the service of a vast, vulgar, and meretricious beauty. (Ch.6)

They were careless people... they smashed up things and creatures and then retreated back into their money or their vast carelessness (Ch.9)

Michaelis saw with a shock that he was looking at the eyes of Doctor T. J. Eckleburg, which had just emerged, pale and enormous, from the dissolving night. "God sees everything," repeated Wilson. (Ch.8)

Theme: Gender and Sexuality

Not even the effeminate swank of his riding clothes could hide the enormous power of that body — he seemed to fill those glistening boots until he strained the top lacing (Ch.1)

I enjoyed looking at her. She was a slender, small-breasted girl with an erect carriage... like a young cadet. (Ch.1)

"I hope she'll be a fool   that's the best thing a girl can be in this world, a beautiful little fool." (Ch.1)

She carried her flesh sensuously as some women can. Her face... contained no facet or gleam of beauty, but there was an immediately perceptible vitality about her as if the nerves of her body were continually smouldering. (Ch.2)

He took what he could get, ravenously and unscrupulously — eventually he took Daisy one still October night, took her because he had no real right to touch her hand. (Ch.8)

Glossary

alliteration	When a **series** of words start with the **same letter** or **sound**, e.g. "held out her hand".
allusion	An **indirect reference** to something else, e.g. Fitzgerald **alludes** to **Keats' poem** 'Ode to a Nightingale' when Daisy claims she **hears** the **nightingale's song** in their garden.
ambiguity	When a **word** or **idea** can be **interpreted** in **different** ways.
American Dream	The idea that **Americans** are **free** to **achieve anything** if they work hard. In the 1920s, the **American Dream** was **linked** to the **pursuit** of **wealth**.
anaphora	The **repetition** of a **word** or **sequence of words** at the **beginning** of **nearby clauses**.
anti-Semitism	A **hatred** of **Jewish** people.
Art Deco	A **style** of **design** that inspired **elegant** and **functional buildings**, **furniture** and **art**.
boom	In economic terms, a **period** of **prosperity**.
bootlegging	**Smuggling** and **selling alcohol** in **secret** during the time of **prohibition** in America.
choric voice	Using, or taking on a **narrative role** that is **similar** to the 'chorus' in **Greek Tragedy** — i.e. **commenting** on the **action** of the **plot**. 'Choric' suggests multiple **voices** speaking together.
consumerism	A **widespread preoccupation** with **buying**, or **wanting** to **buy**, consumer goods.
epigraph	A **short** and **meaningful quotation** or **phrase** at the **beginning** of a **book** or a **chapter**.
feminism	In **literature**, a movement concerned with how **women** are **presented** by **writers**.
flapper	A type of **1920s' girl**, who wore **low-waisted** dresses and had **short hair** — they **challenged traditional expectations** of how women **should act**, e.g. smoking, drinking and having casual sex.
foil	A **character** who **contrasts** with one of the **main characters**, e.g. Wilson is a foil to Tom.
form	The **type** of literature a work is, e.g. novel or poem *or* its **features**, e.g. **structure** or **plot**.
genre	The **type** of **literature** a work is, e.g. **romance**, **gothic**, **detective**, **sci-fi** etc.
Gold Rush	A **large migration** of people to an area following the **discovery** of **gold** there.
Great Depression	The **long period** of **economic hardship** following the **1929 Wall Street Crash**.
hyperbole	Deliberate **exaggeration** that's used to **emphasise something**.
imagery	**Figurative language** that creates a **picture** in the reader's mind, including **metaphors** and **similes**.
irony	When words are used in a **sarcastic** or **comic way** to imply the **opposite** of what they **normally mean**, or when there is a **big difference** between what **people expect** and what **actually happens**.
Jazz Age	The phrase **Fitzgerald** used to describe the period of **prosperity**, **creativity** and **social liberation** in America between **WWI** and the **Great Depression** — it was also known as the '**Roaring Twenties**'.
juxtaposition	Where two things are placed **next to each other** to create a **contrast**.
metafiction	Where a work of **fiction** draws attention to the fact that it's **fictional**.
metaphor	A way of **describing something** by saying that **it is** something else.
Modernism	In **literature**, a movement in the **early 20th century**, in which writers **rejected traditional** literary conventions and tried to **create** something "**new**".

Glossary

motif	A **repeated image** or **symbol**.
myth	A **traditional story** that has **special significance** for the **culture** that it **belongs** to.
narrator	The **speaker** who tells the **story**, usually from their **point of view**.
oxymoron	A figure of speech that **joins** two **contrasting ideas**, e.g. "**elegant** young **rough-neck**".
parody	A **speech** or **work** that **mocks** or **exaggerates** the features of another **speaker** or **literary style**.
pathetic fallacy	When the **weather matches** the **mood** of the scene, e.g. the blazing summer's **heat** during the **conflict** at the **Plaza Hotel** in *The Great Gatsby* **reflects** the **angry emotions** of the characters.
pathos	A quality in a text which arouses **feelings** of **pity** or **sorrow** in the **reader**.
poetic prose	Prose which shares some of the **features** of **poetry**, e.g. **imagery** or **metaphor**.
postmodernism	A **late-20th-century** movement which explored traditional tensions between **high culture** and **low culture**, and argued that 'reality' **changes** depending on **perspective**.
prohibition	A **ban** on **making**, **selling** and **transporting alcohol** which existed in **America** between **1920** and **1933**.
protagonist	The main **character** of the **narrative**, e.g. **Gatsby** is the **protagonist** of *The Great Gatsby*.
Realism	A **writing style** that tries to give the impression that it **faithfully represents reality**.
recession	A period of **shrinking economic activity**, resulting in **high unemployment**.
retrospective narrative	When the **narrator** writes in the **present**, discussing **events** that have **already happened** in the **past**. The narrator may move **between** the **past** and **present tense** to add moments of **hindsight**.
rhythm	A **pattern** of **sounds** created by the **arrangement** of **stressed** and **unstressed syllables**.
Romanticism	A **movement** which began in the 18th century which valued **beauty**, **nature** and the **individual**. This is **different** from **romantic** (with a lower case r) which means relating to **love**.
satire	A kind of writing that **makes fun** of an **individual**, **society** or **politics** to **highlight** certain **flaws**.
sibilance	The **repetition** of 's' or 'sh' sounds in words.
simile	A way of **describing** something by saying that it's **like** something else.
speakeasy	A **place** where people could **illegally buy** and **drink alcohol** during **prohibition**.
stereotype	A set of **ideas** about what a **certain social** or **cultural group** is like.
symbol	An **object** that **stands for** something else, e.g. Tom Buchanan's car is a symbol of **wealth**.
synaesthesia	An **intentional confusion** in a description of the **senses**, e.g. "**yellow cocktail music**".
synonym	A **word** that has a **similar meaning** to another word and could be used as a **substitute**.
tone	The **mood** or **atmosphere** suggested by the **words** the writer uses.
tragedy	A **literary genre** that explores the **meaning** and **impact** of **human suffering**.
tragic hero	The **protagonist** of a **tragedy**, who **struggles** against the **gods** or an **unfair society**, and on **failing**, **dies**.
Wall Street Crash	**Collapse** in the **value** of **shares** in New York, 1929, that triggered a **worldwide financial crisis**.
World Series	A major league **baseball competition** held in America.

Index

Further Reading

It's a good idea to get yourself familiar with the writers Fitzgerald was inspired by. And you can bring critics' views into your essays to support your argument — you don't need to agree with their opinions as long as you can say why not.

Selected Works by Fitzgerald

This Side of Paradise, 1920

The Beautiful and Damned, 1922

The Diamond as Big as the Ritz, 1922

Tender is the Night, 1934

The Diamond as Big as the Ritz is a short story that would be good to compare to the excesses of wealth in The Great Gatsby.

Influences on Fitzgerald's Work

Joseph Conrad, *Heart of Darkness,* 1902

T.S. Eliot, 'The Waste Land', 1922

John Keats, 'Ode to a Nightingale', 1819

Gertrude Stein, *Tender Buttons: Objects. Food. Rooms,* 1914

Biographies

Matthew Bruccoli, *Some Sort of Epic Grandeur: The Life of F. Scott Fitzgerald,* Hodder and Stoughton, 1981

Andrew Turnbull (ed.), *The Letters of F. Scott Fitzgerald,* Charles Scribner's Sons, 1963

Critics

These books contain some of the **essays** discussed in **Section 5**, but they're full of other **useful** things — there'll be a **chapter** or an **article** on **everything** you've ever **dreamed** of. If you dream of **writing** an **essay** on *The Great Gatsby.*

Ronald Berman, *The Great Gatsby and Modern Times,* University of Illinois Press, 1994

Harold Bloom (ed.), *Major Literary Characters: Jay Gatsby,* Chelsea House Publishers, 1991

Judith Fetterley, *The Resisting Reader: A Feminist Approach to American Fiction,* Indiana University Press, 1977

This book contains R.W. Stallman's essay 'Gatsby and the Hole in Time' (1955) and Richard Godden's 'Glamor on the Turn' (1982).

Ross Posnock, '"A New World, Material Without Being Real": Fitzgerald's Critique of Capitalism in the Great Gatsby'. This essay can be found in Scott Donaldson, *Critical Essays on F. Scott Fitzgerald's The Great Gatsby,* G.K. Hall, 1984

Lionel Trilling, *The Liberal Imagination: Essays on Literature and Society,* Secker and Warburg, 1951

William Troy, 'Scott Fitzgerald: The Authority of Failure' (1945). This essay can be found in Harold Bloom, *Bloom's Modern Critical Views: F. Scott Fitzgerald,* Chelsea House Publishers, 2006

Edmund Wilson, *Letters on Literature and Politics, 1912-1972,* Routledge and Kegan Paul, 1977

Films

Watching these films will help you get to grips with the **plot** of the novel.
It's also interesting to see how **directors** have **interpreted** the novel's
ambiguous elements. Grab your popcorn and take a look at some of these...

The Great Gatsby (1949): Directed by Elliott Nugent

The Great Gatsby (1974): Directed by Jack Clayton

The Great Gatsby (2000): Directed by Robert Markowitz

The Great Gatsby (due out 2012): Directed by Baz Luhrmann

Who's Who in 'The Great Gatsby' Cartoon

You should be an expert on The Great Gatsby *by now. But if you want a bit of light relief and a quick recap of the novel's plot, sit yourself down and read through* The Great Gatsby — The Cartoon...

Jay Gatsby

Nick Carraway

Daisy Buchanan

Tom Buchanan

Jordan Baker
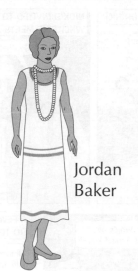

George Wilson

Myrtle Wilson

Meyer Wolfshiem

Catherine

Dan Cody

F. Scott Fitzgerald's 'The Great Gatsby'

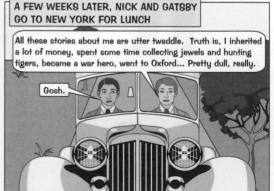